Beating the Odds

Beating the Odds

Eddie Brown's Investing and Life Strategies

To: Will,
Congratulations on your inclusion
in the RECENT "Black ENTERPRISE."
Blessings on your JOURNEY!

Eddie Brown 12/9/11

Eddie Brown
with
Blair S. Walker

WILEY

John Wiley & Sons, Inc.

Published by John Wiley & Sons, Inc., Hoboken, New Jersey.

Published simultaneously in Canada.

For general information on our other products and services or for technical support, please contact our Customer Care Department within the United States at (800) 762-2974, outside the United States at (317) 572-3993 or fax (317) 572-4002.

Wiley also publishes its books in a variety of electronic formats. Some content that appears in print may not be available in electronic books. For more information about Wiley products, visit our web site at www.wiley.com.

Library of Congress Cataloging-in-Publication Data:
Brown, Eddie (Eddie C.), 1940-
  Beating the odds: Eddie Brown's investing and life strategies/Eddie Brown.
    p. cm.
    Includes index.
  ISBN 978-0-470-93662-7; ISBN 978-1-118-06132-9 (ebk);
ISBN 978-1-118-06130-5 (ebk); ISBN 978-1-118-06131-2 (ebk)
  1. Brown, Eddie (Eddie C.), 1940- 2. Investment advisors–Florida–
Biography. 3. African American businesspeople–Florida–Biography. I. Title.
  HG4621.B76 2011
  332.6092–dc22
  [B]
                                2010053518

Printed in the United States of America

10 9 8 7 6 5 4 3 2 1

This book is dedicated to the memory of my grandmother, Mamie Magdalene Brown, a remarkable woman whose discipline, sacrifice, and unconditional love got my life on this planet underway in spectacular fashion. Grandma, you're largely responsible for the man I am today. I hope you've been able to bear witness to some of the things I've accomplished since your untimely death, and I hope I've been able to make you proud.

This book is also for my loving and highly intelligent daughters Tonya and Jennifer, as well as for their extraordinary mother. Sylvia, we've enjoyed nearly half a century of marriage and I love you today with the same intensity and passion that I felt during our college days. My most noteworthy wealth-building achievement has nothing to do with dollars and cents, because I've been rich since the day you agreed to be my life partner.

Last, but certainly not least, I'd like to dedicate Beating the Odds to my precocious grandsons Elias, Benjamin, and Darrell Jr. If you guys take nothing else from this book, I hope the following lesson sticks: If you carry yourselves with dignity and integrity and always give 150 percent to whatever endeavor you happen to be engaged in, I think you'll all be impressed with how things turn out.

Contents

This is a true story, so a few names have been changed.

Prologue

Why me?

I've asked myself that question a million times in the eons since I graduated from Howard University in Washington, D.C.

You see, someone I didn't know from Adam's housecat decided to foot the total bill for my undergraduate education, enabling me to earn a bachelor of science in electrical engineering at the age of 20.

That generosity propelled a kid who once transported illicit liquor onto a path that saw me eventually create a multi-billion dollar money-management business.

Remarkably, my benefactor's generosity came without provisos or conditions. There were no demands about maintaining a requisite grade point average, pursuing a specific major, entering a given field after college, or even forwarding sporadic progress reports while I was at Howard.

I'd love to know what thought processes triggered the life-altering philanthropy set in motion by that mysterious white woman.

So in some ways, *Beating the Odds* is a paean to a now-deceased benefactor I'll always wish I had properly thanked for her largesse, but never did due to the obliviousness of youth.

My other reason for writing *Beating the Odds* is to tell a crackling good tale filled with valuable nuggets about life, the labyrinthine world of investing, and my successful quest to become a philanthropist in my own right.

I'll be dispensing hard-won lessons absorbed over the course of an existence that's presented me with some wonderfully gratifying twists and turns, as well as occasional heartache and heartburn.

Chapter 1

Who Says Talk
Is Cheap?

Y ou haven't lived until you've had 10 minutes to persuade six total strangers to give you $40 million.

It's an incredibly intense exercise, one that definitely heightens your senses and crystallizes your thinking. That's because each passing minute is worth $4 million.

And it's a mission that I'll be embarking on in about thirty seconds.

My name is Eddie C. Brown and I'm in the high-pressure, no-excuses business of managing other peoples' money. Welcome to my world.

Not surprisingly, the eagerness, trepidation, and exhilaration buffeting my innards have me practically abuzz with adrenaline. Even though at the moment I appear to be casually strolling through a Sacramento conference room, I feel like I could just as easily be moon walking across the ceiling!

Onlookers see the approach of a bespectacled, nicely dressed gentleman who is the very picture of competence, confidence, and

1

probity. At least, that's how I hope the six conservatively dressed businessmen scrutinizing my every move view me. I flew here from Baltimore to impress upon them the following: They can't find a more savvy and level-headed soul to safeguard their $40 million, while managing it in a way that yields even more money for them.

The year is 1990 and my audience is the investment committee of the California Public Employees Retirement System, or CalPERS. After I take 10 minutes to lay out my rationales and investing methodologies, then I'll have 10 additional minutes to sagely and succinctly answer whatever queries the committee members may have.

My Baltimore-based company, Brown Capital Management, has been in existence for seven years now and has $80 million under management. In the future, that figure will grow to be billions. But at this point in my corporation's life, I could really use CalPERS' capital, not to mention the credibility that an association with them will confer.

All I need is for the next few minutes to go according to plan.

The CalPERS team regards me with dispassionate, unreadable expressions as I march toward the U-shaped table where we'll be doing business. There's no "Nice to meet you" and "How was your flight?" small talk as I stride toward my fate; only cool, evaluative silence.

Every one of my inquisitors is already seated and ready to get down to business. Wow—these boys are not playing! I can almost hear their thoughts as I smoothly set down my briefcase and prepare to sit myself. *Is he really as good as his financial results indicate? Are we in the presence of a superbly trained, uber money manager? Or a potential time bomb who'll make us look like rank amateurs?*

Numbers don't lie. My clients have historically enjoyed results that have beaten the stock market year after year. However, folks who entrust you with millions of dollars need to be swayed by who you are, as much as by what they read about you on paper. It's time for me to become one of the financial industry's leading purveyors of charm, expertise, and gravitas.

It's time to sell the heck out of my brand.

No sooner does my backside settle into a chair at the conference table than a huge black digital stopwatch with big red numbers on it starts running. Taking note of that simple fact has eaten up two of my precious 600 seconds. This leaves me with nine minutes and fifty-eight seconds to convince CalPERS that I'm their man.

After the 10 minutes for my presentation have elapsed, the CalPERS committee will get an additional 10 minutes to ask questions. Given the amount of money at stake, naturally I've left nothing to chance. I know precisely what I'm going to say, as well as how and when I'm going to say it. I've rehearsed my lines ad nauseam and have literally timed them to the second.

So I let the verbiage I've chiseled into my brain start to flow, and also make it a point to swivel my head so that I can have eye contact with each CalPERS team member.

I start off by thanking them for this wonderful opportunity to compete for their business, and make it clear that I'm intimately familiar with CalPERS' mission, its unique money-management needs, and am eminently qualified to comprehensively address those needs.

As I stop to take a breath, time continues to tick away. The unrelenting digital clock indicates that I have **8:33** left. So far, my spiel is going exactly as I've rehearsed it. I'm excited and revved up, but not nervous because thorough preparation always puts me at ease. Plus in a manner of speaking, I don't feel like I have anything to lose—I've yet to gain the $40 million I'm seeking, so it's not mine.

8:31. Time to launch into a brief history of Brown Capital Management and my 13-year background in the financial industry. This includes having worked for T. Rowe Price, having made regular appearances on the PBS program *Wall $treet Week with Louis Rukeyser* and having earned an M.B.A. from Indiana University. I even toss in a little Hoosier joke, to show these guys they're not dealing with some humorless financial automaton, but an engaging human being they'll enjoy interacting with.

6:47. Of the six CalPERS committee members, three are nodding and smiling faintly, two are expressionless and one appears to be disengaged for reasons that I pray have nothing to do with me. Without missing a beat I begin pulling out visual aids—charts and graphs—and segue into my investing philosophy, which I call GARP, an acronym for growth as a reasonable price. I've got everybody's attention now, even my disengaged friend's.

:10. After hearing only my voice for the better part of 10 minutes, I'm mildly startled when the investment committee chairman pipes up: "Mr. Brown, you have 10 seconds!" Smoothly summing things up, but at a lightning pace, I bring my presentation to a well-choreographed close. And then I take a much-needed breath.

That's got to be the fastest 10 minutes I've ever experienced in my life. The digital clock is instantly reset to tick off 10 more minutes.

Incredibly, the second 600-second allotment flies by even quicker, as the committee members ask questions based on my presentation. Professional athletes often talk about being in the zone when they're really on top of their game. Well, I'm here to tell you that financial professionals sometimes reach that same exalted place as we go about our business.

Before I realize it, 10 more minutes have flown by. I quickly collect my charts and graphs, give each CalPERS member a quick smile and a nod and walk away from the table.

The CalPERS team has several more money managers to interview who also want CalPERS to allocate $40 million to their firms. All of the hopefuls have survived a rigorous vetting process to make it to the interview round, and CalPERS has limited everyone to 20 minutes to ensure that interviews are handled quickly and efficiently.

I leave the conference room feeling totally at ease and satisfied with my performance. Whatever happens moving forward, I'll know that I left no verbal stone unturned in pursuit of CalPERS' $40 million. To use another time-worn phrase from the realm of athletics (my last one, I promise!), I left everything between the lines.

Now that my 20 minutes are over, I feel talked out. I call my wife, Sylvia, to let her know the meeting is a done deal, things seemed to go well, and that I'm on my way to Sacramento's airport for a flight back to Baltimore. And then I get off the phone, perfectly content not to utter another syllable until I'm back on the East Coast.

Bottom line, a few weeks later I get the $40 million dollars I flew to Sacramento for. It was definitely a satisfying victory, and a well-deserved one for my 10-minute speech. Not bad for someone who used to drive moonshine-laden hotrods through the dusty back roads of rural Apopka, Florida, as a youngster.

As soon as the CalPERS money is wired to Brown Capital Management, I immediately call Sylvia and tease her that my time is now worth $240 million an hour, and she needs to treat me accordingly. Given that there's no letup in the honey-do lists tossed my way at home, I guess my playful boast didn't impress her unduly.

So was snagging the CalPERS account my greatest triumph thus far? Not by a long shot. My greatest triumph will always be the way my wife, our two daughters, and I were fortified by God's grace to survive a cancer scare that rocked our tight-knit family to its core.

Don't get me wrong—securing $40 million thanks to a well-executed 10-minute spiel is terrifically gratifying, and I remain very proud of that accomplishment. But money has never been my lord and savior. I've made lots of it in some fairly unique ways and have spent lots in pursuit of altruistic aims and objectives. All over the course of an existence filled with quite a few noteworthy scenarios and challenges.

Chapter 2

The Big Three
to the Rescue

Scientists love to argue whether nature or nurture is the main driver of human development.

During my earliest days on the planet, nurture clearly got the nod.

That tends to surprise people, because when I entered this world in Apopka, Florida, on November 26, 1940, I was the son of a 13-year-old unwed mother.

Folks furrow their brows when I disclose this, undoubtedly envisioning my youthful mom, Annie Mae Brown, balancing me on her hip as the two of us make our way through a cold, uncaring world. Interesting imagery, even if it's off the mark.

The fact is that I enter this life immensely blessed, thanks to three bedrock adults who collectively make sure little Eddie Carl never wants for food, shelter, love, a solid work ethic, intellectual stimulation, adventure, and entrepreneurial training most M.B.A. students would envy.

I call these stalwart personalities the Big Three, and they envelop me in their protective embrace after my mother flees Apopka at the age of 15, no longer able to deal with the stigma of having borne a child out of wedlock.

First and foremost among the Big Three is my de facto mom, Mamie Magdalene Brown, my mother's mom.

Dig into the backgrounds of most successful people who come from nothing and you'll usually find a key person in the background whispering: "You're worthy." "You're capable." "You're destined for greatness."

That's my maternal grandmother. A good-looking woman who is on the short side and plump, Grandma brings an abiding love and stability to my life the likes of which I haven't experienced since her death. I will go to my grave adoring her.

Grandma's stoic, hard-working spouse who's 21 years her elder, Jake Brown Sr., is my father, as far as I'm concerned. A medium-sized man who's bald on the top of his head, has salt-and-pepper hair on the sides, and seems to possess a million sets of denim bib overalls, Granddad isn't big on verbalizing stuff like his feelings for me, or how I should carry myself in life. He just uses every minute of every day as a teachable moment and lets his actions convey what verbiage never does. I don't think I'll ever meet anyone with a purer devotion to work than Granddad.

He's a laborer in one of Apopka's many citrus groves, where oranges, grapefruit, and tangerines are grown. Grandma works as a laborer in a nursery producing philodendrons and other green, leafy plants.

After working brutally long days, my grandparents come home to their second fulltime job of being my parents. I'm often asked if my mother left a void in my life after she departed Apopka when I was two. No, because I was always awash in a sea of unconditional love despite her absence.

My grandparents have another child older than my mother— five years, to be exact—whose name is Jake Brown Jr. Uncle Jake gets his hooks into me a few years after my birth and encourages me to always view life differently than most people, and to never, ever, sell myself short. Uncle Jake also teaches me to unfailingly go after, and expect to attain, the very best life has to offer.

It's Uncle Jake who gives me my first job and simultaneously teaches me how to drive not long after I turn six. He has a crew of migrant workers, primarily from Georgia and Alabama, who come to Apopka in early fall when it's time for the citrus crops to be harvested.

These workers spend the entire harvest season living in five modest, wood-frame dwellings owned by my enterprising uncle. He farms the laborers out to the white owners of large citrus groves scattered around Apopka and is compensated very handsomely for providing seasonal labor.

Uncle Jake owns several trucks that are used in conjunction with the annual harvest, and teaches me how to operate one with its throttle on the dashboard, because there's no way my short legs can operate the accelerator or brake pedals. As I drive the truck down the rows of citrus trees, dwarfed by the huge steering wheel I'm maneuvering, Uncle Jake's workers take heavy boxes filled with fruit and dump it onto the bed of the truck.

I never get paid for my driving duties, which definitely enhances my shrewd uncle's bottom line. But do you think I care? I'm six years old and successfully operating a truck! That's reward enough in itself.

★　★　★

By the way, if you're wondering where Uncle Jake and I get our entrepreneurial gene from, it's my grandfather. At one point in his life Granddad owned 200 acres in a small town west of Orlando known as Ocoee, making him that central Florida hamlet's biggest landowner.

He's forced to flee for his life in 1920, in the wake of a voting dispute between blacks and whites that spawns a gun battle that leaves two whites dead. Afterward a white lynch mob kills nearly 50 blacks and burns down homes and businesses on the black side of Ocoee. Granddad relocates to Apopka, and he never utters a single word to me about his harrowing Ocoee experience. Nor does he ever display a scintilla of bitterness.

My innate passion for hard work didn't come from my biological father, Jeremiah Williams, who was a nonentity in terms of my development. I had absolutely no interaction with him until I was much older, and when we finally did meet the encounter was such a nonevent that I don't recall much about him, or even when—or where—we met.

He wasn't that much older than my mother, meaning he was also young and immature when I was born, Unfortunately the passage of time failed to help concepts like "responsibility" and "accountability" make much of an impact on his carefree, responsibility-shirking brain.

★　　★　　★

The town where I was born, Apopka, is about 12 miles northwest of Orlando and is firmly wedged between Jim Crow's talons during my childhood.

There's a black side and a white side of town and pretty much zero interaction between the two except on Saturdays, when blacks walk to the white side of town to shop for food or clothes. The clothing stores have dressing rooms, but they're for white patrons only. If you're black and try on any article of clothing, you've automatically bought it!

It sounds like a cliché, but the demarcation line between Apopka's two encampments is a set of railroad tracks.

The black side of town is without electricity, paved roads, and running water. That last omission holds particular significance for me, because it means I grow up having to use outhouses whenever Mother Nature beckons.

Even as a child, the notion of taking care of essential business inside a rickety, odiferous wooden shack that's short on privacy offends my sensibilities!

I'm not sure where this "highfalutin'" outlook comes from, given the generations of black Southerners who've spent their entire lives dealing with the elements, ticks, spiders, and snakes whenever a bathroom visit is in order. But I can tell you that even now, I will not frequent a Port-O-Potty because of the flood of disgusting memories those smelly things unleash. Yuck.

Aside from shopping excursions, the only other time I spy whites as a child is during infrequent trips to Orlando, the big city, to visit department stores or to receive medical attention.

My youthful social antennae don't pick up any antipathy or tension between blacks and whites, nor do I detect much curiosity about whites coming from my fellow black Apopka residents. We have our schools and they have theirs and it just seems perfectly natural that in a burg of only 2,000 people, blacks and whites have no contact with each other.

Part of Jim Crow's sickness is the institution's peculiar ability to anesthetize and desensitize, making the patently absurd seem perfectly ordinary and unremarkable.

Chapter 3

The Prince of Apopka

Mortality and death are difficult concepts for 12 year olds to wrap their brains around. So the huge pine tree I'm hurtling toward at 70 mph isn't capable of blasting me and the hotrod I'm driving into smithereens.

The massive evergreen is merely a landmark, the midpoint of a sweeping right-hand turn on an unpaved Apopka, Florida, road I'm zipping along, generating a magnificent rooster tail of tan dust in my wake. That always happens when I pilot the rip-snorting cars Uncle Jake uses to haul moonshine.

Straining slightly, because my legs are barely long enough to fully depress the 1950 Ford coupe's hefty clutch pedal, I brake gently and downshift. The car's tail flicks out a tad as I skillfully maneuver the vehicle's huge, two-spoke steering wheel.

The green Ford's flathead V-8 engine barks a louder, more bellicose exhaust note as I sail through the corner, veering ever closer to the left side of the narrow road where the hulking pine patiently awaits any miscalculation on my part.

But I've performed this move so many times that I could nearly pull it off blindfolded. I'm on my way to wash the Ford, one of 12 moonshine-mobiles Uncle Jake keeps stashed around Apopka. After the car is clean, I'll gas it up and return it to its hiding place.

Accompanying me and smiling like a Cheshire cat is my friend Monkey, so named because of his uncanny resemblance to a howler monkey I saw in an elementary school textbook.

"G'wan Pee Wee, you crazy! YOU CRAZY!" hollers Monkey, a strapping boy whose yellow teeth glisten in the fading evening light.

Even though it's a Saturday and Monkey and I have no school, I'm wearing a freshly-ironed, blue short-sleeve cotton shirt, and khaki shorts that look almost new. One of the nice things about being an only child is never receiving hand-me-downs. One of the bad things about it is always looking like a freshly-scrubbed, black Lord Fauntleroy.

As my buddy and I zoom down the bumpy, rut-filled road, Monkey's large, surprisingly muscular body jounces up and down on the car's bench seat, as does my more diminutive frame.

It's 1952 and passive restraint systems such as auto seatbelts have yet to be invented. Ditto airbags. Actually, Uncle Jake's Ford does have one passive restraint—an unyielding, metal dashboard. It will definitely impede mine and Monkey's forward progress in the event of a crash, provided we aren't ejected from the vehicle first.

Sporting a grin every bit as wide as Monkey's, I shoot him a quick glance. "If I'm so crazy, Monk, why are you here?"

I'm no heedless daredevil. People like that don't skillfully operate high-performance cars at the age of 12. Nor do they grow up to create companies that meticulously manage billions of dollars for very demanding, highly vigilant clients.

I've been driving since I was six, got my first car a year before this when I was 11, and have committed every square inch of Apopka's roads to memory. To include the raggedy, crater-filled ribbons of dirt on the black side of town, as well as the billiard-table smooth black asphalt on the white side of the railroad tracks.

I've navigated this winding road hundreds of times, including while hauling heavy containers brimming with precious white lightning. So not only is there a method to my so-called madness, but also a much-rehearsed routine.

As we hightail it toward the black section of Apopka, I'm exactly where I love to be—coolly assessing and controlling a situation most would find daunting. To ratchet up the degree of difficulty slightly, but mostly to get a rise out of Monkey, I give the Ford a little more throttle.

Bellowing indignantly, the hotrod kicks out its tail at a more pronounced angle, causing us to sail through a curve practically sideways while doing a graceful power slide.

I steal a glance at Monkey whose smile has abruptly vanished, triggering a delighted, high-pitched giggle from me.

"Ain't you worried about cops, Pee Wee?" Monkey blurts anxiously. "You ain't got no license!"

Even though I've taken this curve much faster, I ease out of the throttle for Monkey's sake. Can't afford to rile up the main laborer for my little money-making ventures around town.

"Uncle Jake paid off Apopka's police force," I note matter-of-factly. "They won't bother us."

Nor am I worried about being accosted by rival moonshiners, or the black gamblers and ruffians who flock to Apopka from neighboring central Florida towns every weekend.

Uncle Jake is a legend around these parts, a womanizer who could sweet talk the fur coat off a raccoon, as the saying goes.

When my mom, Annie Mae Brown, headed off to South Carolina two years after my birth, Uncle Jake was more than happy to fill that void. He basically dotes on me as if I'm one of his children.

My relationship with Uncle Jake has an element of parent/child to it, but it goes a lot deeper than that.

To my impressionable 12-year-old eyes—and I'm not trying to be blasphemous—Uncle Jake is practically the Second Coming!

Tall, slender, and dark-skinned, his two front teeth rakishly framed in gold, my uncle is one of the most dominant personalities in Apopka, which proclaims itself the "Indoor Foliage Capital of the World." Even though he never went beyond sixth grade, Uncle Jake has never worked for anyone a day in his life.

Despite that, he lives a life filled with money, prestige, fast cars, fast boats, and women so fine that other men regard my uncle with a degree of admiration bordering on awe.

Uncle Jake runs legal and illegal businesses with the aplomb and sure-handedness of a Fortune 500 CEO. None of this is lost on me—I'm always furiously scribbling mental notes whenever I'm around him.

As Monkey and I hustle down the road, a neatly-folded $1,000 bill with Grover Cleveland's image on it is securely nestled in the right front pocket of my khaki pants. One thousand 1952 dollars is roughly equivalent to $8,000 in 2010 currency.

At least one day every week, Uncle Jake hooks me up with my friend Grover. I never tell Monkey when Grover's on the scene, because Monkey has a bad habit of blabbing everything he knows about a second after he knows it.

Sometimes I introduce Grover to some of Apopka's prettiest girls, including a flirtatious 15 year old whose older boyfriend glares at me like he'd love to kick my ass. He probably senses that his girl and I have done some heavy-duty petting behind his back.

It's all part of a modus operandi I picked up from my uncle. Even though he has a beautiful and loving wife, Aunt Nadine, at home, Uncle Jake also has a string of mistresses around Apopka. And at least one love child that I know of.

Some of Uncle Jake's outside women have boyfriends, and even husbands. But no one in Apopka messes with Jake Brown Jr., placing a wonderful protective halo around his emulative little nephew.

Even though I've never seen Uncle Jake physically harm anyone, Apopka's roughest black males always seem to adopt a deferential tone in my uncle's presence.

This includes the thuggish Boot Mouth, a foul-tempered, ornery son of a gun with a proclivity for kicking men in the face if they don't repay his usurious loans quickly enough. Boot Mouth might be tempted to draw his foot back at me if he knew how often I casually tote around a thousand dollars.

Uncle Jake entrusts me with Grover to ensure that I'll be comfortable around wealth, instead of intimidated by it.

But he's also sending an unmistakable message: "This kind of money can be yours if you work for yourself, instead of the backbreaking, low-paying labor most of Apopka's black citizens perform in area citrus groves and plant nurseries."

It's a message I've taken to heart: Basically, I want to be exactly like Uncle Jake in every conceivable way, to include his generosity, his positive outlook, his no-nonsense work ethic, and even his suave, serial philandering.

And as soon as I'm old enough, I'll keep a loaded .44-caliber revolver tucked in my waistband, just like my idol.

"Pee Wee, lemme drive," Monkey says in a wheedling voice after the road straightens out. "I drives good!" That's a bald-faced lie, as we're both well aware!

The bulk of Monkey's "driving" has taken place inside parked cars, while he makes goofy engine noises with his mouth. It seems uncharitable to mention this, given that I've already been driving for six years.

"Monk, let's just get this thing washed," I say, making my friend poke out his lips and silently glare at a dense forest of evergreen trees that's beginning to give way to citrus groves and fields filled with corn and other crops.

The stench of hogs begins to waft intermittently through the Ford's open windows, because we're leaving the forest and entering South Apopka, the black side of town. It wouldn't be accurate to say it's a one-stoplight place: No-stoplight is more like it!

Even so, South Apopka is a bustling, vibrant locale with a surprising number of businesses and hole-in-the-wall entertainment venues.

South Apopka is the hub of my youthful universe, where I happen to live an odd man/child existence. On the one hand, I get stellar grades in elementary school and ride my bike and enjoy playing marbles and baseball like Apopka's other black boys. Conversely, thanks to Uncle Jake, I'm exposed to activities like running moonshine and frequently find myself in settings where I'm the youngest person present, as well as the only one not packing a knife or pistol.

★   ★   ★

"Pee Wee, let Lucinda see our car," Monkey says, following what for him is a world-record embrace of silence. Without asking for permission, he turns on the radio, unleashing music from a rectangular speaker on the dashboard.

Lucinda is a homely sixth-grader Monkey thinks is cute. For me, doing Uncle Jake's bidding is a trillion times more important than helping Monkey impress Lucinda.

"Maybe next time, Monk," I answer over the din of engine noise, music from the radio and hot, humid air rushing through the car's open windows. "Uncle Jake wants us to finish, but I tell you what— instead of paying you 15 cents for helping me wash four cars, today you get 20."

Monkey turns to see if I'm serious, which I am. I start slowing the Ford, eventually creeping along at 20 mph. It feels like I could run faster, but it's bad form to fly through black Apopka while simultaneously kicking up a dust blizzard. Anyway if some kid were to accidentally ride his bike in front of me, there's no way I could stop on this dirt road.

As we glide along, I spot a tiny blue, one-story wooden house ahead. The modest dwelling is dwarfed by a huge oak tree with dainty-looking, lime-green Spanish moss dangling from its limbs.

That's where I live with my grandparents.

"Duck down, Monkey!"

My buddy obediently slides out of sight onto the Ford's bench seat, as I briefly accelerate to 35 mph and look away from my grandparents' house as I pass.

If they see me driving one of Uncle Jake's moonshine cars, a lot of questions will ensue that neither my uncle nor I will want to deal with.

Then I won't be able to drive Uncle Jake's fleet of speedsters or hobnob with Grover Cleveland. And when Uncle Jake, the King of Apopka, holds court in the town's juke joints and gambling venues, the precocious Prince of Apopka will be banned from joining him.

I couldn't stand not being able to shadow my mentor, watching him routinely perform deeds that most people around here wouldn't have the moxie to think up, much less execute.

Fortunately, my grandparents are nowhere to be seen as I rumble by. Monkey and I drive to the home of one of Uncle Jake's associates and pump bucket after bucket of well water in order to get the Ford sparkling clean.

While Monkey dries the car with a towel, I prop up the hood and stare at the engine. I have no idea what the strange-looking plumbing and wires do, I just know that Uncle Jake has somehow managed to wring 120 horsepower from an engine that came from the factory producing only 100.

No one has taught him auto mechanics, either. He just intuitively knows how to take apart a complex auto engine and reassemble it in an improved state.

Rounding out Uncle Jake's eclectic skill set, not only does he make managing 25 workers toiling in a citrus grove look easy, but he's able to calculate their payroll—as well as what he's owed for overseeing them—using some kind of mental calculator.

Even animals aren't immune to Uncle Jake's charms. He gets a kick out of training the squirrels around his house to eat food from his hand and to ride on his shoulders.

Now you tell me—what 12 year old could resist falling under the sway of a life force as powerful as Uncle Jake's?

After the Ford is washed and refueled, and after an ecstatic Monkey has gotten his 20 cents and been dropped off at home, I sashay about a mile in the dark along a dusty road. You have no idea how absolutely pitch black night can be until you've been on a country road without an electric light in sight. That's because the black side of town isn't wired for electricity.

Thanks to my overly active imagination, every time a bird calls out, or a leaf rustles in the nearby woods, I quicken my pace. By the time I hit the final half mile, I'm practically jogging!

My shirt is drenched with sweat when I reach my grandparents' home. Knowing that this will further annoy Grandma, who likes me to be in the house well before the sun sets, I quietly enter the chicken coop near our home.

The pungent smell of chicken poop assaults my nostrils as I open the door, then check under each hen for eggs. Since I'm late, may as well greet my grandparents bearing gifts. As I go from hen to hen in the dark, I silently say a little prayer each time: "God, please don't let me accidentally grab a snake!"

I've collected three eggs from hens irritated at being manhandled after sundown, when out of nowhere comes a faint roar. It quickly grows louder—an eight-cylinder engine approaching from the south at an awesome clip. I'm guessing anywhere from 90 mph to 100 mph.

Taking care not to crack the eggs in my hands, I push open the chicken coop door and sprint into the dirt driveway beside my house. Pretty soon a rumbling white Plymouth appears, followed by a cyclone of dust and wind.

Uncle Jake coasts a few feet beyond the driveway, then the Plymouth's backup lights illuminate as my uncle slowly parks in the driveway. The only time he backs into driveways is when he's carrying moonshine.

Beaming, I run toward the driver-side door and encounter the bracing aroma of Uncle Jake's cologne before I reach him. He's ditched his work coveralls for a snazzy blue vest with white pinstripes, covering a crisp, long-sleeve white shirt.

"Boy, whatchoo doing out here?" Uncle Jake booms as he opens the car door and gives me an affectionate pat on the head. "You done my cars?"

The door to the house opens and I see the plump figure of my grandmother, who's wearing a loose-fitting cotton floral dress and clutching a lantern.

"I just finished," I inform my uncle urgently. "I haven't been in the house, yet."

Immediately sizing up the situation, Uncle Jake grins and rubs a large hand over my close-cropped hair. "You just rode up here with me!" he says, drawing a one dollar bill from his billfold. My uncle gently stuffs the money into the pocket of my wet shirt.

"Thank you, sir!" I tell him, feeling a tremendous surge of pride. I shift the three chicken eggs into my left hand, pull Uncle Jake's thousand dollar bill from my pants pocket and ceremoniously present it to him.

"I took good care of Grover for you," I say, looking up into my uncle's chiseled, handsome face.

Noting the imminent approach of my grandmother, Uncle Jake discreetly makes a fist around Grover without depositing the bill in his pocket.

"I know you do right by me, boy," he whispers. "That's why Grover your friend."

Grandma is upon us now, her face illuminated by her lantern. I don't like her expression.

"Eddie Carl," she says sharply. "Where've you been? Your dinner is cold!"

"He was with me, mama," Uncle Jake interjects. "Washin' my cars."

Grandma looks at Uncle Jake suspiciously, then at me. "Where did those eggs come from?"

Before Uncle Jake can answer, a loud rustling noise comes from the vicinity of an orange grove directly behind my grandparent's house.

"There he is!" a white man's voice yells out. "Git him!"

Moving faster than I've ever seen before, Uncle Jake dives into the open driver-side door of his Plymouth and frantically starts the engine. At the same time, three unfamiliar white men sprint toward the driveway, guns drawn. They're wearing civilian clothes and have badges pinned to their shirts.

"Goddamit, stop boy! Stop!"

Uncle Jake's response is to gun the Plymouth's engine and drop the clutch. Roaring as though possessed, the vehicle fishtails wildly into the road, spraying me and Grandma with dirt.

"Go, Uncle Jake!" I yell out, prompting Grandma to frantically gesture for me to hush. Then she watches helplessly as one of the men runs into the road and draws a bead on her only son with a pistol. Fortunately, Uncle Jake is already so far away that he doesn't present much of a target.

Another car materializes out of nowhere and swerves to a stop in front of our driveway. Sweating and cursing, the three men with pistols pile in and take off in the direction of Uncle Jake's vehicle.

"We'll be back!" one of the men snarls out a window.

Grandma puts one of her strong arms around me and pulls me toward her, as though shielding me from some unspeakable horror.

I'm appalled myself. How could Uncle Jake have been blindsided like this, given all the money he pays Apopka's cops? In any event, the men pursuing Uncle Jake will never catch him. He's too good a driver, his car is too powerful, and he's too doggone smart.

Listening to the fading ruckus of the intense car chase, I secretly fantasize about the day when the revenuers come after me.

When that happens, they'll have even *less* of a chance than they do now, because the Prince of Apopka will have learned his lessons well.

Chapter 4

Death and a Kidnapping

Uncle Jake lies low for a few days following his dramatic brush with the law, which drives Grandma crazy with worry. Then one afternoon he just pops up, going about his ordinary routine and acting as though nothing unusual has happened.

Grandma is so angry that I think she'd finish off what those lawmen started if she had a gun. Neither she nor Granddad discuss my uncle's antics with me, but a couple of times I've come upon them huddled in intense conversation, and I'm pretty sure Uncle Jake was the topic of discussion. Grandma and Granddad always stop talking whenever I approach, which annoys me.

I'm not sure if they think I'll tell Uncle Jake what they're saying, or if they feel I'm not smart enough to interact on their level, but it's insulting either way. Two can play that game, however.

Consequently, I don't say a word to my grandparents after my uncle takes me aside and shows me how his pursuers got close enough to shoot out the back window of his white Plymouth.

My silent admiration of Uncle Jake puts me in a distinct minority in my grandparents' household. To my way of thinking, Uncle Jake is merely using his ingenuity and mother wit to carve out an existence superior to the depressing, back-breaking, hand-to-mouth existence of most black Apopka residents. Such is the optimism of youth that potential pitfalls such as incarceration, or a bullet to the head, don't even enter my thinking.

I'm pretty sure the appropriate palms in Apopka's law enforcement community have been sufficiently greased, allowing Uncle Jake to not only avoid apprehension and incarceration, but to engage himself once again in the business of running moonshine. It hasn't been lost on me, either, that the scales of justice come in two varieties: One for poor people, and a totally different, more lenient version for those with sufficient cash to purchase the legal outcome they desire.

Now that he's back on the scene, Uncle Jake's rakish *modus operandi* hadn't changed one iota—he still swaggers around Apopka with a confidence bordering on arrogance. He's still very much my hero and I still drive all 12 of his hotrods without my grandparents' knowledge. I've even graduated to the point of sometimes making moonshine deliveries for Uncle Jake.

I'm sure no other kid in Apopka, black or white, leads a dual existence approximating mine. By day I'm getting As in school, which keeps my grandparents happy. At night, I'm hanging out with a rogue's gallery and driving cars capable of hitting 140 mph.

This is the natural order of things, as far as I'm concerned.

*   *   *

Part of me died on July 3, 1955.

When I think back to that day, I'm still struck by the contrast between how prosaically it started, and how irrevocably my life changed by the time it ended.

Grandma, Uncle Jake, and I leave early in the morning to visit my mother. About two years earlier, she began trying to have more contact with me, because we were basically strangers. So I spent most of the previous two summers with her in Allentown, Pennsylvania, where she lives. Looks like this is going to be the third summer in a row I'll be spending time in Allentown.

The sun isn't up yet and it's already 80 degrees on July 3, 1955, as I leave for Allentown in a car driven by Uncle Jake. Grandma, who's never been to Allentown, is accompanying us.

Uncle Jake's driving his Chrysler family sedan, instead of one of his 12 hopped-up moonshine runners, which are too loud, uncomfortable, and way too fast for the business at hand.

If it had just been me and Uncle Jake on this journey, he'd let me drive, because I operate cars like a pro at 14. I should be a proficient driver, in light of the fact that when I was 11 my uncle gave me a 1936 Ford he'd converted into a pickup truck.

But out of deference to Grandma, who's a straight arrow and never deviates from the rules—especially niggling ones like needing a license to operate a motor vehicle—Uncle Jake does all the driving. As the Chrysler jounces along on its interminable journey to Pennsylvania, I sit alone on the expansive rear seat, bored out of my mind.

To be honest, I'm kind of lukewarm about this whole Allentown deal. If you've been separated from your child for more than a decade, then wait until he or she is a teenager to reintroduce yourself, there's going to be some resulting awkwardness and distance.

That pretty well sums up my relationship with my mom. I don't feel negatively toward her, but I also don't feel the warmth one would ordinarily associate with their mother. Grandma is my mother. My biological mom in Allentown is in many ways like a big sister who's 13 years older.

A sister with a mean live-in boyfriend she always seems to be arguing with, and who makes little effort to hide his disdain for me. Fortunately, I always fall right in with the Allentown boys my age, so that's a positive associated with these summertime sojourns up North. So is indoor plumbing, because Allentown visits spare me from dealing with infernal outhouses!

I'm thinking about this as verdant South Carolina farmland whizzes past the windows of Uncle Jake's Chevrolet. I feel like a caged animal and can't wait for Uncle Jake's next gasoline break.

Grandma must be ready for a rest stop, too, because she can't seem to get comfortable on the seat beside Uncle Jake. She's fidgeting and fanning herself, even though plenty of evening air is streaming into the car at 55 mph.

She turns to my uncle, and I see her face is glistening with sweat. "It's so *hot*. I feel like I'm gonna faint! Stop, so I can get some water." My grandmother never complains about anything, so her words and urgent tone instantly get my attention, as well as Uncle Jake's.

"What's wrong?" my uncle inquires, looking quite concerned.

"I dunno. I'm so thirsty!"

Hearing fear in Grandma's and Uncle Jake's voices, I lean over the front seat and turn toward my grandmother.

"Do you need me to do something?"

Grandma shakes her head "no" and makes a brave attempt to smile, but fails to mask her grimace. Uncle Jakes pulls off the highway as soon as he can, and he and I frantically start looking for a house with black people near it.

They'll be able to point us toward a medical facility where Grandma can be treated. Medical emergencies are no excuse for black people to suddenly materialize at white southern hospitals during the height of Jim Crow.

"I caint hardly breathe," Grandma says, panic driving her voice up a couple of octaves.

Uncle Jake sees some black kids playing in front of a house up the road, and comes to a sliding stop in the dirt driveway. I put my hand on Grandma's trembling shoulder, but she doesn't acknowledge it.

"Getcha mama!" Uncle Jake bellows out the window, and the children obediently scurry off. They return with an alarmed looking young black couple in tow. Uncle Jakes hops out and intercepts them before they reach his Chrysler.

"Where's a hospital?" my uncle asks imploringly as he points to Grandma in the front seat. The young black man jogs back inside, while his wife rapidly strolls over to our Chrysler to investigate.

"Water, honey!" Grandma says weakly, perspiration now darkening the top of her floral dress and making her hair stick to her face. Something in my grandmother's expression and demeanor convey an instant sense of urgency to the young woman. She runs back inside her modest wooden frame house and returns with a glass of water and chunks of ice wrapped in a paper towel.

The kindly woman holds the glass of water for Grandma, who takes teeny birdlike sips. Grandma's angel of mercy then tenderly holds the ice-packed paper towel against my grandmother's forehead. I watch this standing outside the car, as a mysterious force clenches and unclenches something in my abdomen.

The young father runs out of his house and starts his car, and Uncle Jake and I jump back into our vehicle. Both cars fly down the road at breakneck speed for about 15 minutes, until we reach a nondescript-looking, two-story wooden structure abutting a heavily forested lot. The black hospital.

Uncle Jakes dashes inside, leaving me in the car with Grandma, whose eyes have rolled back into her head and who's mumbling and grunting incoherently and is now totally drenched in sweat.

"Everything's gonna be alright, Grandma," I tell her in a quavering voice. "You'll be okay." That's really a positive affirmation for my benefit, because by this point she can't hear me.

Uncle Jake, a black nurse, and an orderly pushing a gurney come flying out of the hospital, quickly load Grandma onto the gurney and whisk her inside. For a split second Uncle Jake just stands and watches, his gangly arms hanging loosely at his sides. I see something in his face I've never seen before or since: Total helplessness and abject fear.

My uncle offers to give the man who led us to the hospital a couple of dollar bills, but he graciously declines, so my uncle and I enter the hospital and are directed to a laughably small waiting area containing three tattered chairs and a battered wooden coffee table.

We wait there for the next three hours, pacing the floor when we get tired of squirming in the uncomfortable chairs. Finally a stocky male doctor who looks to be in his late fifties enters the waiting room, and Uncle Jake and I immediately stand before him. I take one look at the doctor's expression and immediately know what the deal is.

The beloved woman who anchors my world is no longer with us. Sure enough, the doctor tells Uncle Jake: "I'm very sorry, but your mother passed from a heart attack. We tried to save her, but it would have taken a miracle."

Neither my uncle nor I speak. We just clutch each other and stand in the middle of the waiting room floor and weep inconsolably, as successively larger waves of shock and grief crash down over us.

Afterward, I pretty much cease functioning. I'm glad Uncle Jake steps up like the strong man he is, because I'm a numb, grieving wreck the rest of the day. I keep thinking about how Grandma had never been up North before, and how excited she was about going to Allentown, Pennsylvania.

Allentown! If she had lived longer, I would gladly have sent her to Cape Town and Brisbane and Buenos Aires and Paris. And Allentown, too, if that would have made her happy.

Before Uncle Jake and I leave the hospital, he goes back to where they'd been working on Grandma and takes one last look at her, something I have zero desire to do. Then he drives us to a black funeral home and arranges to have Grandma's body shipped back to Apopka. Once that's taken care of we head back south, retracing our tracks from earlier in the day.

We ride in pained and disbelieving silence in the same car where Grandma had been chattering excitedly a few hours earlier about seeing Allentown for the first time. And now my 54-year-old grandmother is gone forever. It doesn't get much more surreal.

At some point, Uncle Jake must have called Granddad and passed along the tragic news, because Granddad gives me a stiff, teary-eyed hug in the driveway of his house following the long trip back to Apopka.

I immediately burst into tears and run into the house, leaving Granddad—who now looks older than his 75 years—standing in the driveway. He probably needs solace as much, if not more, than I do. But like most 14 year olds, I'm primarily focused on my own well-being.

If there was a member of the Big Three who was irreplaceable, it was Grandma. Uncle Jake stokes my sense of adventure and my entrepreneurial side, while Granddad is a dependable rock who's full of stoic affection.

However, I enjoyed a magic connection with Grandma I'll never have with Granddad or Uncle Jake. Boys typically have a sacred bond with their mothers, and Grandma and I definitely had ours.

When someone very close to you dies unexpectedly, the shock is quadrupled if you have to be in a setting where you interacted with that person every day. Grandma's presence permeates every square inch of my grandparents' nicely furnished, two-bedroom house, and every time I turn a corner I see or touch something that triggers a cascade of poignant memories.

Like the used upright piano sitting in a corner of our living room. Grandma bought it on her menial laborer's salary so I could take piano lessons with Mrs. Gladden. Every time I look at that oak-colored musical instrument, tears start falling.

Same thing with the black Underwood typewriter she purchased, and then taught me how to use by paying a lady down the street to give me typing lessons. I really took to typing, and can still dash off 60 words a minute to this day.

Typing was part and parcel of Grandma's desire for me to get a good education, and then work in a white-collar setting. That was her two-pronged game plan for me. It was made crystal clear that I wasn't to work in one of Apopka's ubiquitous plant nurseries and citrus groves, like she and Granddad did.

Whenever I pass through the kitchen, which is still filled with heart-tugging cooking aromas, I can still see Grandma stoking the wood-burning stove and conjuring up finger-licking meals. Stuff like rabbit and fried fish served up with grits, collard greens, black-eyed peas, and lots and lots of gravy.

The kitchen is also where I saw Grandma feed hungry individuals. Folks from Apopka, as well as non-residents, have sat at our table and were personally served home-cooked meals by my grandmother.

Memories like that are why I shed most of my tears in the kitchen.

Mamie Magdalene Brown was such a strong, loving force that I feel totally lost without her. It would be nice to share my feelings with someone, but Monkey lacks the intellectual depth and maturity to grasp what I'm experiencing. Uncle Jake is busy dealing with Grandma's funeral logistics, and I don't have strong enough emotional ties with Granddad to broach any of this. Anyway, he's sort of floating around in shock himself, having just lost his longtime mate.

When the day of the funeral arrives, I sleepwalk through the entire affair at St. Paul A.M.E. Church in Apopka. To this day I can't tell you what the weather was like or who attended. I've had a lifelong knack for purging unpleasant things from my memory banks, and I honestly think that talent stems from my grandmother's death.

Next to the date Grandma passed away, the day of her funeral is the second-most painful of my young life. I'm glad when it finally comes to an end.

Nature abhors a vacuum, so it's said, and Grandma left a whopping one that Uncle Jake smoothly fills. Not because he has any ulterior motive, but simply because he loves me deeply and sees that I'm adrift and in intense pain.

I begin spending more and more time with my uncle, and take on more and more responsibility within his moonshine-running enterprise. Everything we do together seems to be an adventure, including the simple act of getting together. That can't take place until Granddad dozes off in the evenings.

He sleeps like a rock, so it's a simple matter for me to sneak out of the house as soon as his rhythmic snoring starts rocking the rafters. From that point forward I'm free to hang out with Uncle Jake late into the night. Given that I'm well into pubescence and my male hormones are rumbling, why wouldn't I want to be around the beautiful women who frequent my uncle's orbit?

Unknown to me, my nocturnal activities with Uncle Jake are being closely monitored. Not only that, but the person doing the watching—an adult second cousin named Lillie Mae Moore who lives next door to Uncle Jake—isn't amused.

A few months after Grandma's funeral, Cousin Lillie Mae places a call to Allentown. She tells my mother that my burgeoning relationship with Uncle Jake and his questionable circle of associates has me on a surefire path to delinquency. Possibly even damnation.

Cousin Lillie Mae urges my mother to come to Apopka and scoop me up while I can still be saved from replicating my uncle's incorrigible ways.

So one day after I leave my eleventh grade high school class, I get the shock of my life. As I walk into my grandparents' house, who should be sitting at the kitchen table but my mother! Granddad is sitting with her.

"Lillie Mae has been telling me about you spending a lot of time with your Uncle Jake," Mom says, getting straight to the point. "Lillie Mae thinks he's a bad influence. So I'm going to take you back to Allentown to live with me."

I look to Granddad for a reprieve and he silently gives me a barely perceptible shrug. My mother's word is law, it appears. To her way of thinking this is probably a noble rescue operation. So why does it feel more like a kidnapping?

We're off to Allentown tomorrow morning, courtesy of Greyhound. I can say good bye to Granddad, Uncle Jake, moonshine, sauntering around Apopka with $1,000 bills, my entire way of life. This includes a diverse array of entrepreneurial endeavors that provide me with multiple income streams.

At the age of 14, the Eddie Brown, Inc., umbrella covers a firewood sales business, which calls for me to collect discarded slabs of wood from a nearby lumber mill. Two days a week I also water plants around the home of a man who owns a local citrus grove. I get paid a dollar and a half a week for that, and give Monkey a quarter for doing most of the work.

On Saturdays I work as a bootblack cleaning and shining shoes on the black side of town. Another money-making enterprise is a small plant nursery I've built behind Uncle Jake's house. Monkey and I also pull Spanish moss from trees and sell the moss by the pound to people who use it as stuffing for pillows and furniture.

Also, if Mom goes through with this Allentown transfer, I'll be waving bye bye to Hungerford High School, a segregated school I attend in nearby Eatonville, Florida, because the high school in Apopka is for whites only. Right now any grade I achieve less than an A is unsatisfactorily low for me, so surely my mother isn't serious about uprooting me from Apopka, given all the fascinating and positive things I'm immersed in here?

Since Granddad clearly isn't going to intervene on my behalf, when I say my prayers prior to going to bed, I petition God to make my mother change her mind and let me stay in Apopka.

Apparently He's on Mom's side, too, because the following morning I find myself hunkered down in a Greyhound seat alongside my mother, starting the long bus ride to Pennsylvania's third-largest city.

Chapter 5

Magnificent, Mysterious Lady B.

I'd mentioned earlier that when I lived in Apopka, nurture was the main factor shaping my development, as opposed to nature. A reversal of sorts occurs not long after I move to Allentown.

It shouldn't come as a surprise that I don't arrive in Allentown in the best frame of mind. Not only am I still grieving over Grandma, but I'm very displeased with the manner in which I've been spirited out of Apopka.

I've been abruptly yanked out of my comfort zone, something I'll do intentionally and frequently later in life. Because by then I figured out that the biggest upticks in personal growth usually come on the heels of turning your life upside down and shaking it vigorously.

But not yet having the wisdom of age and time, I'm a brooding, sullen presence for about the first month after my arrival in my new hometown of Allentown. Being passive-aggressive becomes the safest way to express my displeasure and annoyance with Mom, unless I want to run the risk of having her slap the taste out of my mouth!

Ours has never been a cozy relationship to begin with, so throwing in a little undercurrent of volcanic resentment hardly sweetens the mix. To Mom's credit, if she takes note of my sulking or is annoyed by it, she never lets on.

Looking beyond my consternation, it's great to be living in a blue-collar, industrial city that's devoid of Whites Only signs for bathrooms and drinking fountains, an odious practice that was the norm in central Florida. Not too far from downtown Allentown are nice stores and movie theaters I can actually patronize without worrying about a Jim Crow double standard.

There are also sweet shops, little stores frequented by both black and white kids that serve soda pop and ice cream, and that have a juke box and a dance floor in the back.

Blacks are in the minority in Allentown, meaning there are far more white girls my age than black ones. However, in the more racially tolerant North, I can now gaze upon any girl without fear of retribution from a more narrow-minded public.

It's telling that being able to fraternize with white kids doesn't strike me as a big deal. It strikes me as normal, and I quickly get used to the racial status quo in Allentown, as opposed to Apopka.

Even in settings where integration is firmly entrenched, blacks and whites still tend to gravitate to their own race out of comfort and familiarity, and 1955 Allentown is no exception. Mom lives in a black part of the city that, in retrospect, wasn't a very nice section of Allentown.

It's not crime-ridden or anything like that. It's just that the rowhouse and the entire block where we live are clearly run down and have seen better days. As I previously mentioned, there's running water for an indoor toilet, but no hot water for a bathtub or shower. I still have to take baths in a big corrugated metal tub after the water is first heated on a stove, just as in Apopka.

But at least Mom has electricity, which black Apopka incredibly still lacks a full decade after the end of World War II!

Even though Mom's only 27, she's lost most of her teeth as a result of skirting the dentist's office and then getting periodontal disease. So she wears false teeth that she takes out at night.

She's a couple of inches shorter than my five-foot-eight height, and not plump like Grandma. Mom's placid demeanor reminds me of Granddad in that she's slow to anger and even slower to articulate any other emotions she may be feeling. I don't get a lot of hugging and kissing and verbal encouragement from her, like I got from my demonstrative Grandma practically on an hour-by-hour basis.

I often find myself wondering if Mom would have sent for me if Grandma were still alive?

Unfortunately for me, my mother's loutish boyfriend—Calvin—is still on the scene. I'd fervently hoped he'd be gone by the time I got here. A man who carries bricks to bricklayers at construction sites, Calvin looks to be about 15 years older than Mom.

They say consistency is the hobgoblin of small minds, which explains why Calvin is every bit as boring, dull, and mean as I remembered him. I haven't been in Allentown 24 hours before I resign myself to the reality that I'll probably never receive a scintilla of intellectual stimulation or kindness from Calvin.

If anything, he resents my presence even more than during my summer visits, because now I'm in Allentown permanently. His intolerance is ironic, given that Calvin's son from a previous marriage, Calvin Jr., lives in our rowhouse, too.

Junior is an aggravating, immature little pest who's about two years younger than me and who practices his trumpet around the house in a way that sounds like a flatulent goat. Calvin Jr. relishes proudly informing everyone he meets that I'm his big brother. To which I invariably reply: "You're not my brother!"

Which always prompts him to say, "Yes I am!" and for me to shoot back, "No, actually you're not!" Little Calvin probably thinks I'm joking around, but I couldn't be more serious.

I've been an only child my entire life and have no burning desire to suddenly share the spotlight with the goofball offspring of my mother's detestable boyfriend. At least Calvin Jr. has a more outgoing, high-energy persona than his father, which isn't saying much since a loaf of bread exudes more charisma and magnetism than Calvin.

*   *   *

In the 1950s United States, many people presume that all things Southern and African-American are inherently mediocre and second-rate, until proven otherwise. Consequently, the administrators at my new school, Allentown High, automatically want to place me in an industrial arts curriculum, given that I've been attending an all-black high school in Eatonville, Florida, which is just outside Apopka. Adding insult to injury, they presume that even though I was in the eleventh grade in Eatonville, I can't possibly be up to speed when it comes to Allentown's public-school curriculum. So, they want to push me back to tenth grade.

Most people don't know that the black community had an incredibly gifted and dedicated cadre of teachers during segregation times. These educators were on a mission and they pushed and molded black kids relentlessly, but also with tremendous caring and skill.

Mom knew this from having attended all-black Southern schools herself, even though she never went beyond junior high. She also knew from talking to Grandma, and to me, that academics were the least of my worries and that my Eatonville teachers have prepared me quite well to excel academically, starting from when I entered elementary school.

My mother deals with my education situation in a way that's so out of character that it literally startles me. Basically, she accompanies me to school and very forcefully and indignantly informs my principal that I will not be taking industrial arts classes, and I will not be repeating tenth grade.

Out my huge class of 754 students, only seven of us are black, and I'm sure the principal has never encountered a black parent as assertive and self-assured as Mom. He hems and haws in the face of her verbal onslaught. But darned if my mother doesn't prevail. I never take an industrial arts class, nor am I set back a grade. Instead, I take eleventh-grade college-prep courses, at Mom's insistence, and become one of the top students in my class, just as I was in Eatonville.

So once I overcome the artificial impediments laid down by my high school's administrators, with my mother's help, my educational transition actually plays out pretty smoothly.

I still play baseball with the boys and now have a cute blonde girlfriend who has no interest whatsoever in pursuing higher education. Her main goal in life appears to be hanging around Allentown after high school, and having a good time, so it's very clear to me that we'll never advance beyond the high-school sweetheart stage.

I've also joined an all-black gang whose grandiose moniker is *The Fabulous Kings*. We sport pink jackets with The Fabulous Kings embroidered on them, black pants with a pink band near the pockets, and square-toe black and white shoes. As you probably gathered from our sartorial splendor, The Fabulous Kings are far from juvenile delinquents. Rather, we consider ourselves lovers and musicians, and can usually be found singing doo-wop songs on Allentown sidewalks most evenings.

Collectively the Kings have above-average talent, and even travel to New York City every now and then for minor singing gigs. I've taken to tootling on a saxophone and can honestly say that my meager playing skills don't go a long way toward elevating The Fabulous Kings' musicianship. But boy am I having fun! With each passing day, Apopka, Granddad, and Uncle Jake fade a little further into the distance. So does the tremendous heartache associated with Grandma's passing.

Something else that's been relegated to my past is the entrepreneurial activities I pursued in Apopka. I'm making money in Allentown, but it's through having little after-school menial jobs that generate spending change. It keeps me from having to mooch money from Mom, which I'm sure pleases Calvin to no end.

Unknown to both of them, I've been diligently saving my money. I've always been very disciplined when it comes to establishing financial goals, along with budgets to support them. That discipline will be the foundation for my livelihood later in life. But for the time being, it's helping me inch toward something I desperately want to acquire.

Saving is a difficult thing to do when either Calvin or Calvin Jr. are always floating around the house. Uncle Jake taught me not to be too trusting of people where money is concerned, and I took that lesson to heart.

So part of my savings are stuffed in my school locker, while the rest can be found in a hiding place in Mom's teeny backyard.

By the time the summer of 1956 rolls around, I have enough socked away for a down payment on a 1950 Ford. When I ask Mom if she'll sign the financing paperwork, she does so unhesitatingly, since I'm not usually wheedling and begging for money and material things.

Also, she knows my Ford significantly improves the transportation picture in our household since she doesn't drive.

Personally, I like the added independence that comes from having my own wheels. Several of my Allentown friends have cars and I don't care for always having to bum a ride when I need to go somewhere. So the summer of 1956 makes me a car owner once again, a privilege I first got used to at the age of 11.

There is one small problem—won't turn 16 until November, so I have to drive my Ford in accordance with the restrictions found on a Pennsylvania learner's permit.

The Ford represents something else—it marks the first time I've set a long-term financial goal. My car proves to me that in the future, financial objectives can be attained by handling money in a responsible, disciplined fashion.

★   ★   ★

On a sad note, 1956 is also the year Granddad makes his transition and joins my beloved grandmother. To my way of thinking, I basically attend the funerals of my mother and father in consecutive years.

Jake Brown Sr. is 76 when he passes away, and I guess some might say he lived a very full life, given that the average life expectancy for an American male during the 1950s is sixty five and a half years.

However, I'll always be convinced that Granddad died of a broken heart, because Grandma's death seemed to greatly diminish his enjoyment of life.

Once my senior year of high school starts, I return to being one of the top students in Allentown High School. I'd like to go to college, but have no clue what I would study, what school I would go to, or how in the world I would pay my tuition.

I just have this notion that college is somehow in my future. Grandma always said that if I didn't want to make my living in some Apopka plant nursery, covered head-to-toe with itchy brown muck, that higher education was the way to accomplish that.

Mom, on the other hand, is telling me that whatever I want to do with my life is fine with her. She does not exert any influence one way or another.

Given that I'm doing particularly well in math and science, one of my high school guidance counselors suggests that I take a test that might give a sense of what profession I might be best suited for. When I go back to the counselor's office for my results, she says the test result indicates I might want to consider becoming an engineer.

"What's that?" I ask, genuinely baffled. I've never met an engineer and have no inkling what they do.

Instead of looking surprised or condescending, the counselor just smiles. "Eddie, engineers build things," she says. "And they rely heavily on math and science to do it. Your car, the road you drove on this morning, even the school's steam boiler were all designed and built by engineers."

I let this revelation sink in for a second, and think back to an electronics kit I bought over the summer. For some reason I got interested in Morse code and built a little radio that allowed me to communicate with people in faraway places in Morse. It was fun.

"Do engineers work with electronics?" I ask hopefully.

"Yes. There's a field of engineering called electrical engineering."

So over the course of a 15-minute visit to the counselor's office, I decide that I'm going to become an electrical engineer. When I was in Florida, one of my teachers at Hungerford High School used to rave on and on about her alma mater, a historically black college in Washington, D.C., named Howard University, and how much she enjoyed it.

I never bothered to ask what impressed her so mightily about Howard, but based on her glowing endorsement, Howard is the only school I submit an application to. It never occurs to me to apply to other schools, in case I'm rejected by Howard.

Pretty dumb in retrospect, but what do you expect from a 16-year-old who's trying to become the first member of his family to attend college?

It seems the higher-education gods are smiling on me, because Howard admits me. I often wonder what would have happened if I hadn't taken that aptitude test steering me toward engineering? Or if one of my teachers hadn't suggested Howard? Or if Howard had rejected me, without me having a safety school as a backup?

Now that I'm one-for-one in the college-admission game, there's a minor fly in the ointment: How am I going to pay for my education? Mom, who works as a maid for white Allentown residents, doesn't have the wherewithal to take on Howard's room and board. I'm sure Uncle Jake would gladly subsidize my education, but unfortunately his lifestyle choices have finally caught up with him and he's serving a one-year prison sentence in Florida.

One day I happen to casually mention my financial-aid dilemma while talking to one of Allentown's black community leaders, Sylvester Rone. I met him while working as a bootblack in downtown Allentown, and Mr. Rone took a shine to me from that point forward . . . no pun intended.

Of the handful of black students who are about to graduate from Allentown High School, most have their sights set on jobs at local construction sites, or with one of three manufacturing firms located in Allentown.

"So what do you want to study at Howard, young blood?" Mr. Rone asks as we stand in front of an Allentown department store where I've run into him.

"I want to be an engineer, sir," I inform him confidently. "I'm going to major in electrical engineering, so I can help build radios and televisions."

"That a fact?" Mr. Rone asks, laughing as he eyes me carefully. "What makes you think you could do that?"

"I don't know, sir. But I put together a Morse code radio from scratch, and I used it to communicate with people in North Carolina. So I know I can do it."

"I might be able to help you, Eddie," Mr. Rone says slowly. "But you have to promise that you won't let me down if I do. You a man of your word?"

I look Mr. Rone directly in the eye, so there can be no mistaking my sincerity. "Yessir."

"Tell you what. I hear through the grapevine that a white Allentown businesswoman is lookin' to send a black kid to school. College. Tuition, room and board, everything." I immediately start smiling because, even without additional details, a warm feeling washes over me—a solution to my college-expenses problem has just materialized! I don't have a clue why I feel this way—it's one of those intuitive hunches you get in life every now and then and can't explain.

Mr. Rone tells me what the woman's name is, but I don't remember it. What does stick in my mind, however, is that she owns a casket-making business. I laugh when he discloses this, because it strikes me as an incredibly bizarre way to make a living.

Ultimately, Mr. Rone says he'll bring my situation to the casket lady's attention, and makes me swear that I won't embarrass him if my prospective benefactor—who I've taken to calling Lady B., the B is short for benefactor—agrees to subsidize my college plans. Then he tells me to write down what college I plan to attend, what my major is going to be, and so on, and he'll pass it along. So I write down the information Mr. Rone requests on a sheet of lined notebook paper, hand it to him, and then practically float home with excitement. Mom is in the kitchen of our rowhouse, frying Polish sausage while her lug boyfriend, Calvin, loiters impatiently, waiting for dinner to be prepared. I immediately tell my mother about my conversation with Mr. Rone and am disappointed and baffled by her lack of excitement, as well as by her obvious skepticism.

Calvin is even more straightforward. "Annie Mae, dis boy supposed to be smart, heh?" he smirks. "Then why he still believing in fairy godmothers? You evah seen a cracka lookin' to send jigaboos to college?"

My mother momentarily stops stirring the sausage in the frying pan and frowns, but says nothing as Calvin laughs uproariously. I do not find his observation remotely humorous.

I'm tempted to ask if he has any forward-thinking ideas for securing my Howard financial aid, but that would only come off as impertinent and disrespectful. Anyway, I know full well that if I never set foot on Howard's campus, Calvin won't lose a minute of sleep over it.

When I say my prayers prior to going to bed, I ask God to put me in a situation where Calvin will wind up eating his negative words.

The following day, I don't see Mr. Rone. Or the day after that. Nearly a week goes by before I reconnect with him, again, as I happen to be walking through downtown Allentown. He rushes over to me and wraps me up in an elated bear hug.

"She's gonna do it, young blood!" Mr. Rone exclaims, bouncing happily on the balls of his feet. "It's all taken care of—all you need to do is go to class!"

With zero fanfare—and working through an intermediary, no less—my surprise benefactor, Lady B., has decided to bring me into her orbit.

I'm curious if she's checked into my background, to ensure that her money isn't going to a future Howard University party animal, or someone who might not make it through freshman year. Does she ride around Allentown in a chauffeured limousine, secretly spying on me as I work as a bootblack? Does she listen surreptitiously as I sing doo-wop on street corners, and has she arrived at the conclusion that my musical talent needs to be augmented by higher education?

I don't have the answers to any of those questions. That's because I never request a one-on-one meeting with Lady B. It was a youthful mistake that I'm not going to beat myself up over too badly, either, because if she wanted to meet with me that could have been facilitated quite easily. All she had to do was tell Mr. Rone and he gladly would have set things up.

Still, I should have been more proactive and assertive in terms of learning more about Lady B. and her interest in me and my education, as well as in terms of thanking her.

Regardless of that oversight, Lady B.'s intervention into my life was a huge deal for a couple of reasons. Obviously, I might never have attended college were it not for her.

But also because she introduced me to a brand of philanthropy that in some ways mirrored Grandma's kind act of feeding the hungry in the kitchen of her Apopka home. Lady B. filled me with a burning determination to get to a level in life where I could do for others what she did for me.

Chapter 6

Engineering a
New Existence

It's August 1957 and I'm moments away from driving my 1950 Ford from Allentown to Howard University to begin school. I've never been to Washington, D.C., or stepped foot on a college campus, so this is a morning of firsts.

"Good luck, Eddie," my mother says in the living room of her rowhouse. Calvin is also present and is wonderfully silent, no doubt enjoying the sweet taste of crow after negatively predicting my mystery benefactor would turn out to be wishful thinking.

"Do a good job, study hard, and make good grades," Mom continues in a flat, unemotional voice, in keeping with her personality. Then she hugs me hard and I'm out the door, on my way to my car, which holds a trunk stuffed with my clothes. I've also loaded my blue Ford down with math books, which are my favorite things to read at this stage in my life.

It takes me about three hours heading down U.S. Route 1 to reach Washington, D.C. As I drive, I marvel at the sinuous path my life has followed in only 16 years. Two years ago my end all and be all was to be a co-equal with Uncle Jake in his moonshine operation. Now he's in jail and I'm headed to college to become an engineer, with all of my educational expenses magically paid for.

I've experienced more in 16 years than many adults do over the course of their entire lives, and I seriously doubt Howard can serve up any surprises I can't cope with.

The school has a reputation of being one of the best historically black colleges in the United States, so I'm excited about the prospect of meeting lots of intellectually inclined black kids. I've also heard Howard has a lot of good-looking women and that the male/female ratio is definitely in my favor, so I'm excited about that, too.

I'm impressed, and more than a little awed, the minute I turn onto Howard's campus. I hadn't expected it to have so many large, multi-story buildings! And because Howard's in the city, I hadn't anticipated so many broad swatches of pretty green grass. Plus, it takes all of 10 seconds to see that Howard has just as many spectacular coeds as advertised.

I manage to locate Cook Hall, my dormitory building, and am shown a small third-floor room I'll share with one other student. But for me, the real moment of truth comes after I make my way over to Howard's registrar's office.

"My name is Eddie Carl Brown," I inform a kindly looking black woman behind the front desk. "Ma'am, uh, is my tuition and everything taken care of?" I feel butterflies tickling my stomach as the woman steps away and retrieves a manila folder, then walks back to the front desk and sits down.

Sure enough, Lady B. has forwarded a check for $1,000 that takes care of tuition, room and board, and books for my entire freshman year. I can't help but see a parallel between this and the days that Uncle Jake used to let me walk around Apopka with a $1,000 bill, as if that were some kind of precursor.

Incredibly, I don't have to submit progress reports to Lady B. or even maintain a minimum grade point average. All I have to do is go to class. I feel fortunate to have such an effortless scholarship, and seriously doubt that any other student attending Howard has a sweet financial aid arrangement comparable to mine.

I immediately feel at home at Howard and have no problem acclimatizing myself to the school's academic and social demands. I absolutely love this environment—it's clear to me that I was born to be a college student. Something about the pursuit of knowledge galvanizes me, and I have always had a thirst for learning.

Howard is an oasis of intellectual stimulation, whether it's being provided by an incredibly bright cadre of accomplished and conscientious professors, or by a student body that represents the crème de la crème of upwardly mobile young African Americans. In and out of the classroom, I'm continually finding myself participating in conversations that challenge and engage me.

Something else is at play here that goes deeper than mere education. At Howard and other black colleges and universities around the country, education is viewed as an indispensable weapon in the fight for civil rights and economic parity. So there's an undercurrent of earnestness to everything that goes on at Howard. Yes, there are students who are frivolous, carefree hedonists primarily looking for a good time or a mate, but they're in the minority.

Being a focused and responsible type, I sometimes feel the hopes and dreams of an entire race are riding on my narrow young shoulders, and that I'd better make full use of the incredible opportunity that's fallen into my lap. Another student who appears to have the same outlook, and that I become fast friends with, is Bill Bell, a fellow freshman electrical engineering major who goes on to become a multi-term mayor of Durham, North Carolina.

Starting school at Howard marks the first time in 10 years that I don't have to work to earn money. My only job is to learn to the best of my ability and I'm gratefully generating grades that catapult me to the dean's list.

The icing on the cake is the fact that Howard's social scene is downright magical. The campus fraternity with the largest number of swashbuckling members is Omega Psi Phi, so that's the one I join. I'm into a pattern of hitting the books hard Sunday through Friday, and then fully enjoying the party circuit Friday and Saturday nights.

I even manage to pull Howard's freshman queen, Tamara Ewell, a lovely young lady who becomes my girlfriend. Dating the freshman queen has elevated me to a whole new social strata, one that I don't necessarily like. Tammy enjoys the limelight, while I've never been one to draw attention to myself. More shy and retiring than I care to admit, I don't like walking around with a bull's-eye on my back. Not only are a lot of guys going after Tammy, but I've become some kind of trophy for a lot of the young ladies. Two qualities that have always served me well—a knack for time management and an ability to set priorities—come to the fore.

I start putting less time and energy into my relationship with Tammy and shift the pendulum toward academics. My engineering course load is starting to kick my butt, and I find myself studying into the wee hours of the morning simply to stay on top of things, something I've never had to do before. As a result I maintain a sterling grade point average while my relationship with Tammy withers on the vine and evaporates.

Mom hasn't traveled to Howard during my first year, and never visits the campus the entire time I'm attending classes. She doesn't call me and doesn't expect me to telephone Allentown, but we do exchange a few succinct letters and notes. It's not that we don't love each other—ours just isn't your run-of-the-mill mother/son relationship.

When my freshman year at Howard winds down, I'm still on the dean's list and looking forward to spending my sophomore year in an off-campus apartment with engineering student Walter Stroud and two other students. However, my return to Howard is pegged to something I have no control over, and that's Lady B. fulfilling her promise to subsidize my college education.

Whether that happens or not, I end freshman year feeling pretty doggone good about myself. It's clear to me that I can fit in comfortably whether I'm running with intellectuals, street-corner guys singing doo-wop, or rural roustabouts drawn to one of the region's premier moonshiners. It's reassuring to know that I'm capable of being that facile and adaptable. This tells me that not only can I handle whatever life throws my way, but there's a high probability that I'll also prosper. That's my mindset as I head to Allentown to shine shoes and set pins in a bowling alley for the summer.

For a few weeks I hold down a good-paying job digging ditches. But to my chagrin, a friend who got me the position fakes an injury while on our job site, resulting in both of us getting fired.

*   *   *

When August 1958 rolls around, Lady B. does what she pledged to do, and a check addressing all of my sophomore-year financial needs magically materializes in Howard's registrar's office. As I did last year, I write Lady B. a one-page letter thanking her for her once-in-a-lifetime largesse.

At the age of 17, it still hasn't dawned on my young brain that a thank you missive isn't sufficient for expressing my gratitude. It will, but that's a few years off.

Year two at Howard kicks off like year one ended, which is to say I'm inundated with physics, chemistry, and the like. I like courses like these, but what I don't care for are what I disdainfully call soft courses. That term covers electives such as sociology and philosophy and most liberal arts fare. Later in life I will really come to greatly appreciate soft curriculum and what it represents, but for now it's merely an impediment on the path to a bachelor of science degree in engineering.

At some point in the fall semester of my sophomore year, I began dating a ball of fire from Virginia named Sylvia Thurston. Majoring in physical education and health, Sylvia is on the thin side, roughly my height, and is tremendously vivacious and not at all afraid to voice an opinion on any topic.

For example, I've taken to occasionally smoking a pipe at Howard, something I think makes me appear urbane and far worldlier than my 17 years. The only problem with my pipe is that I have a terrible time keeping the darn thing lit, something that amuses Sylvia to no end, for some reason. She's constantly laughing at my self-extinguishing smoking utensil, and nagging me that it's going to wind up giving me lip cancer.

She likes me, and I feel the same way about her. Today after nearly half a century of marriage we still express our enduring affection for each other with curt little zingers and wise cracks, just like during our Howard days.

In college, she's a bit more socially conscious than I am. We're both serious students out to achieve the best grades possible, so we typically try to get together at least twice Monday through Friday, and for a few hours on the weekend. A lot of our dates consist of me taking her in my car to nearby Rock Creek Park, where we enjoy the moonlight and wide-ranging conversation.

I'm the perfect gentleman during these little Rock Creek excursions, although not because I'm any great saint. I'm as interested in earning another notch in my belt as any other teenage boy, but Sylvia puts out a vibe that she's above being a conquest. And I respect that.

Toward the latter part of my sophomore year, the realization comes that I'm deeply in love with Sylvia and may have found my soul mate. God knows that isn't something I was looking for, as if any youthful, footloose male is.

All male Howard students have to take Reserve Officer Training Corp (ROTC) classes during their first two years. Bill Bell and I decide to continue with ROTC during our junior and senior years, too, meaning we'll get a small stipend. We'll also get the gold bars of an Army second lieutenant and a two-year active duty commitment when we graduate.

Not being warrior types, we both choose the Signal Corps when asked what part of the Army we want to be associated with. The Signal Corps deals with electronics and communications and rarely comes directly in contact with combat scenarios, unlike artillery, infantry, and armor.

Our thinking is that it's better to take care of our military obligations as commissioned Signal Corps officers for only two years than to risk the very real possibility of being drafted into an enlisted combat slot for a longer period of time. So Bell and I have military drills once a week while school is in session.

Things are getting darned interesting for me on the personal front, too. I'm pretty sure Sylvia is *the* one, that special person who'll be the mother of my children and who'll loudly snicker when I'm an old man whose pipe refuses to stay lit. While I don't claim to be able to divine what goes on in the female brain, I think she wants to marry me, too.

So my plan is to approach her one-on-one at some special venue, and offer her my fraternity pin. For a guy to give a young lady his frat pin at Howard means that the two of you are engaged for all intents and purposes. Rings and carats and all that expensive stuff can come later.

So during a class break I drive down to Sylvia's parents' house in rural Virginia. When her family's not around and it's just the two of us, I reach into my pocket, dig out my Omega Psi Phi fraternity pin and hold it out to Sylvia with a trembling hand. Instead of jumping up and down and reaching for it, she recoils slightly, then just stands there and looks at me.

After what seems like an hour, she looks at me and says, "No, Eddie. I'm not taking that!" While I don't think I'm God's gift or anything, *I cannot believe she just rejected my fraternity pin!*

It's so awkward and incredibly uncomfortable being around Sylvia and her family afterward that I quickly make some lame excuse to drive back to school. As I head toward Howard, I repeatedly ask how I could have possibly misread things so badly? I also blister my Ford's interior with a few choice curse words, which is unusual for me since I'm not into cussing.

I feel better by the time I arrive back in Washington, D.C. Yeah, I'm still somewhat deflated, but if Sylvia Thurston thinks I'm going to just quietly disappear like some easily rebuffed punk, she'd better think again.

In the fall and spring of my senior year, corporate recruiters flood Howard's engineering school. I'm trying to decide what I'm going to do in terms of a career path once I have my electrical engineering degree. I've given some thought to electric power distribution, but that's not really where my head is. So I've made up my mind to go into electronics, and consequently interview with a lot of electronics companies.

It seems that incurring a two-year ROTC active-duty obligation has its drawbacks, because it's scared off an awful lot of corporate recruiters. Thankfully, at least one company appears undaunted, and that's aerospace giant and major defense contractor Martin Marietta.

They have a huge division in Orlando that makes Titan missiles and they offer me a position down there doing quality control analysis. The compensation is a princely $6,500 per year, and Orlando is a few minutes away from Apopka, my old stomping grounds.

I arrange to get my Army commitment deferred for one year and sign on the dotted line with Martin Marietta. I'm an electrical engi-neer now, because getting my B.S. is just a formality as far as I'm concerned. Anyway, receiving a sheepskin doesn't make my achievement palpable for me, but accepting a job offer sure does.

All of my friends—Bill Bell, Sylvia—are ecstatic when I tell them about Martin Marietta and congratulate me to high heaven. If only they could appreciate just how dramatically I've evolved during my 20-year journey. I can't speak to the one person who would be able to fully grasp that, Grandma. So accepting Martin Marietta's offer of employment is in some ways a bittersweet experience that dredges up aching sensations of loss I'd hoped to never feel again.

Bell is also offered a position with Martin Marietta in Orlando and accepts. We have a parallel universe relationship that started before we met each other, when we independently concluded that attending Howard as electrical engineering majors was the way to go. Now we're going to be working for the same unit of the same company, and have made commitments to be active-duty Army officers for two years.

When June 1961 rolls around, Mom comes to Howard for the very first time to watch me become the first Brown family member to graduate from college. Sylvia, who has one more year at Howard due to being in a five-year program, is also present.

She's the one who pins the second lieutenant bars to my Army uniform during an ROTC ceremony, and afterward when I offer my fraternity pin again, it's accepted this time, followed by a lengthy kiss.

You might think that on the day I receive my diploma, I'd set aside a few moments to dash off a multi-page note to Lady B. to thank her for making this day possible. But I don't.

That's okay, because I'm going to become a philanthropic force to be reckoned with. How I'll do this on an engineer's, and then an Army lieutenant's, salary isn't clear to me. But where there's a will, there truly is a way.

Chapter 7

Europe on Five Dollars a Day

I mentioned earlier that my potential life as a moonshine maven came to a halt because an adult cousin, Lillie Mae Moore, told my mother to remove me from Apopka. When I tell Cousin Lillie Mae that I'm coming to Orlando to work as an engineer with Martin Marietta, she says there's an extra room in her house in Apopka and insists that I stay with her.

So I take her up on that kind offer, but tell her I'll only do so if she allows me to pay rent. Whenever I think about how this living arrangement neatly brings things full circle, I can't help but smile. I'm sure Grandma is smiling somewhere, too.

Cousin Lillie Mae has clearly taken full ownership for the upward arc of my life, because she's been squiring me around Apopka and proudly showing off Eddie Carl as if I were her son. I don't mind, because without her timely intervention there's no telling where I'd be.

Cousin Lillie Mae still lives next door to Uncle Jake, who's no longer the incorrigible scofflaw who prompted my relocation. The year he spent in prison demonstrated to him the error of his ways, because his moonshine enterprise is a thing of the past.

These days he's an upstanding citizen who supports himself solely by supplying migrant labor to Apopka citrus growers. When no one else is around, we reminisce about blasting along the back roads of central Florida while ferrying white lightning. I still admire Uncle Jake, but now it's hard to believe that I once aspired to be his protégé and craved a lifestyle that easily could have gotten me shot or imprisoned. I was a product of my environment.

This is why I go on to create special programs for inner-city kids, and why I empathize with urban youth who've fallen in step with a drug-dealing culture that's surrounded them their entire lives. It's not right and I'm not condoning it, but if that's all you know, it's all you know. I was headed down a similar path once myself, so I'm not going to shake my head and cluck my tongue from on high.

Getting back to Uncle Jake, the moonshine may be gone, but his non-stop womanizing and philandering continues unabated. Again, I don't pass judgment, but I prefer following a different path now that I'm engaged to Sylvia. While Uncle Jake teases me about this, oddly he seems to respect and admire my fidelity.

I'm a few days away from starting work with Martin Marietta in Orlando, and so is Bill Bell, so Cousin Lillie Mae contacts a friend and gets Bell a room about a block from her house. Bell and I work for Martin Marietta for only a few months before we get letters from the Department of Defense ordering us to report for active duty in November.

The reason behind our orders is the Cuban Missile Crisis. Neither I, Bell, nor Martin Marietta are pleased about this development, but what can you do? I didn't have any inkling the world was on the brink of nuclear Armageddon. Like any recent engineering grad worth his or her salt, I'm staying abreast of the latest developments in my field, not reading the front page of the newspaper.

Uncle Sam couldn't care less about my failure to keep up with current events, he just wants Bell and I to report to Ft. Monmouth, New Jersey. So we drive up from Florida, and are absolutely thrilled to discover that Army veterans have dubbed Ft. Monmouth "The Country Club of the East."

The facility is close to the Atlantic Ocean and also not far from New York City. But things get even better after Bell and I report for duty—since we were both electrical engineers, we're given the option of teaching an electronics class to Army enlisted soldiers. Basically an eight-to-five job that keeps us from having to go on field maneuvers and deal with tents, sleeping bags, and so on.

Even though I'm an Army lieutenant, I'm in an educational environment and at one of the most desirable bases in the Army. An aspect of my posting that I don't care for are white soldiers from places like Alabama and Mississippi that don't want a Negro teaching them anything. It doesn't matter that I'm a commissioned officer with an electrical engineering degree.

I had totally expunged that ugly little fact from my memory banks, until Sylvia reminded me of it as I was writing this book. I had also forgotten that during a civilian job I held years later, the Ku Klux Klan held a demonstration march on the street beside my office. Life is full of impediments, with racism being a particularly pernicious one. But I've never been one to focus in on obstacles or to give them undue power over me or my life. If you're driving down a road and there's a huge sinkhole ahead, you can either obsess over its presence—which won't make it go away—or you can map out alternate routes that keep you headed toward your destination.

During my initial months at Ft. Monmouth, one of the main things on my mind is: How do I make the paltry salary of an Army second lieutenant produce enough money to buy Sylvia an engagement ring? One with a diamond she won't need a microscope to see?

One of the beautiful things about military service is how easy it is to save money. You have no overhead to speak of, in terms of healthcare costs, food bills, or rent. Aside from occasionally going into New York City with Bill Bell, I really don't have any expenses to speak of, so by the time December 1961 rolls around, I'm able to purchase Sylvia's ring, in accordance with a financial timeframe I'd established.

When it comes to saving and investing, foresight and discipline are practically always rewarded. I can't think of one instance in my life where that hasn't been the case.

As you already know (since you're reading my book and don't glow in the dark), President Kennedy was able to eventually defuse the Cuban Missile Crisis, pulling the world back from the brink of nuclear annihilation. However, Uncle Sam decreed that Bell and I would still have to serve out our two-year military obligation.

I arrange to get a leave of absence to get married on August 11, 1962. Not surprisingly, I wasn't involved in the planning of my nuptials, which take place in a Baptist church in King William, Virginia. I have two overriding memories of getting hitched—I'm absolutely terrified up to the point of exchanging vows, and no alcohol of any kind is present. That latter fact really riles up some of my fraternity brothers in attendance. The affair is spirit-free because Sylvia's parents, Charles and Carmen Thurston, don't drink. Truly remarkable when you consider that Sylvia is one of four siblings.

I didn't have enough leave, or money, for a honeymoon. So my new bride and I lease an apartment in Asbury Park, New Jersey, not far from Ft. Monmouth. Readily conceding that it will be a while—if ever—before the two of us are featured in *Better Homes & Gardens*, we fill our place with dirt-cheap furniture.

It isn't long before the Brown household has two income streams, because Sylvia manages to nail down a job as a physical education teacher at a nearby middle school. Sylvia's annual salary of $5,000 surpasses mine, which somewhat rankles me for a reason I can't quite put my finger on. I'm now a first lieutenant in the Army, and am not supposed to be making much money, but still . . .

Within a few weeks after entering into holy matrimony, Sylvia is teasing me good-naturedly about two perceived shortcomings. First, she says the name Brown is too run-of-the-mill, so she'd prefer another last name! As if I waited until we were standing at the altar to spring my surname on her.

Her second complaint is a bit more serious, because Sylvia is disappointed to discover that I don't have a handyman gene in my entire body. I never held myself out to be a handyman, so I don't why she's surprised I'm not Mr. Fix-it. On the other hand, Sylvia's father, Charles, has an uncanny ability to fix things, much like Uncle Jake. I may not have that gift, but one thing I do possess is the ability to put together a terrific family budget.

It's gratifying to see that even though Sylvia is more of a spend-thrift than I am, we see eye-to-eye on finances and both have the requisite discipline to make a budget work. I had discreetly sounded Sylvia out on this critically important topic prior to getting married, so I had a pretty good idea we'd be in accord.

Basically, we've just been taking a certain percentage of our combined monthly incomes and socking it away into savings. In the future I'll make hundreds of millions of dollars through picking stocks, but at this point in time I lack the sophistication to know that investing is even an option.

As Sylvia and I begin our new life together, we have some really important things to achieve that call for money. First and foremost is starting a family. We're both on board with that, although when I tell Sylvia that I'd love to have six crumb snatchers, she looks at me as if I'm an extraterrestrial.

We'll need enough money to eventually buy a house at some point. Lastly, and it's not clear to me that Sylvia has fully bought into this financial goal, I need to have the wherewithal to make charitable contributions. Now that I'm married and two years out of college, I'm starting to appreciate the full magnitude of what Lady B. did for me at Howard.

But to be honest, the way Sylvia and I are living paycheck to paycheck, I can't make much of a charitable impact right now. Nor do I ever see that happening while I'm drawing an Army lieutenant's salary.

It may seem counterintuitive, but learning to live within your means is actually superb training for potential entrepreneurs. Because when most people start businesses, capital is usually in terrifically short supply. Knowing how to keep things operating on a shoestring budget is an invaluable skill for someone in the initial phases of running a company.

By the time 1963 rolls around, I'm just waiting for my military commitment to end, so I can get another job as an engineer and start making some real money.

Actually, were it not for a simple eye test, I would gladly entertain the notion of staying on active duty longer than the two years I'm currently on the hook for. I love airplanes and aviation and applied to enter the Army's helicopter flight school at Ft. Rucker, Alabama. But my left eye was found to be marginally substandard on a visual acuity test. Since I can't go to flight school, I'm sticking with my two-year plan.

Before leaving active duty in 1963, I have a particularly noteworthy experience that involves Sylvia. To make up for not being able to take her on a proper honeymoon, on our first anniversary I arrange for us to fly standby to Europe aboard military transport planes.

Bill Bell and his new wife, Gwendolyn, were supposed to go with us, but are expecting their first child. So me and Sylvia—with our dirt-poor, adventuresome selves—travel to Germany, France, Italy, and England, aided by a book titled *See Europe on Five Dollars a Day*. What a fabulous excursion!

It marks the first time either of us has been on a plane, or out of the United States, for that matter. Why is this vacation particularly noteworthy? Well, in addition to being tremendously educational and fun, I'm impressed by the ease with which Sylvia adapts to exotic, stimulating worlds outside her usual frame of reference.

I plan on doing plenty of that in life, and it's reassuring to know that my mate is not only capable of taking the ride with me, but looks as though she'll relish it.

Chapter 8

"Ed, We're Already Doing Okay!"

I've finally figured out what I want to be when I grow up.

It's taken me five years of working as an electrical engineer for IBM, along with earning a master's degree in electrical engineering from New York University, to figure out I no longer want to be an engineer.

What I really want to do is join IBM's management ranks and leave my present position at the company's facility in Poughkeepsie, New York, where Sylvia and I both live. What I really want to do is go back to school and get a master of business administration (MBA). My goal is to attend class fulltime, instead of on a part-time basis like I did when I commuted back and forth between Poughkeepsie and New York City to get my master's in engineering.

Sylvia and I now have a two-year-old daughter, Tonya, lots of incredible friends, a house and a comfortable lifestyle thanks to my IBM salary and Sylvia's compensation as a junior high school teacher in nearby Hyde Park, New York.

To be honest, I'm dreading the hell out of broaching this subject with my wife, because I know it's not going to go over terribly well. The carefree, footloose Sylvia who happily traipsed around Europe with me when I was in the Army has been replaced by a settled, dutiful wife and mother who is more than happy with the nest she currently occupies.

I'm not stupid or oblivious—I appreciate where Sylvia is and I'm not particularly eager to roil the waters in my calm, happy household. There's a lot of validity to the truism that when mama's happy, everybody's happy. But does that mean daddy necessarily has to die a slow, quiet, agonizing death if the status quo doesn't float his boat?

What's my problem at IBM? I don't have one per se, another reason my sales pitch about quitting work to attend school fulltime will be incredibly difficult. Things are going wonderfully for me at IBM's Systems Development Division, where I design computer circuits for large mainframe computers.

It's 1968 and there are people who'd give anything to work for IBM, one of the country's most storied employers. Not only am I securely in Big Blue's employ, but I play a role in creating the corporation's bread and butter product, mainframe computers.

I'm currently designing circuits for the System 360, the largest mainframe in IBM's inventory, and I'm the only black engineer in a small group of roughly 10 people headed by a terrifically smart gentleman named Hironadandi. My group is filled with genuinely nice people and I regard four of them as close friends.

One of the team members has a place on a lake quite a bit north of Poughkeepsie, and he's invited Sylvia and I to go waterskiing several times. My spouse and I discovered that we prefer riding in my co-worker's boat a lot more than tumbling behind it as we do high-speed pratfalls into the water.

The people at IBM are nice, the work is challenging, and I'm being handsomely compensated. Yet I've gotta get out of there, and there's a simple explanation why: The path I'm currently on will never facilitate financial independence. Continuing to work as an engineer for IBM will not allow me to casually write checks covering Tonya's college tuition, and it certainly will never subsidize philanthropy approaching Lady B.'s.

So it's critical that I get on IBM's management track, and the best way to accomplish that is by having an MBA tucked in my back pocket. I began giving that serious thought after stumbling across a Ford Foundation study looking at the nation's top executives and their commonalities. Just about every one of the guys holding down the corner office possesses an MBA.

Not long afterward, I happened to read a *Poughkeepsie Journal* article about a new program seeking to encourage African Americans to go after MBA degrees. Known as the Consortium for Graduate Study in Business for Negroes, the program works in concert with three business schools—University of Wisconsin, Washington University, and Indiana University. The number of business schools would later swell to 12.

If I apply to the Consortium and am selected to participate, the cost of my tuition will be paid by the Consortium, which is funded by the Ford Foundation.

My other option is to apply to one of the three schools acknowledged to have the best business programs in the country, Harvard, Stanford, and the University of Pennsylvania's Wharton School. My tuition will not be subsidized if I do that, and the cost of any of those schools will easily wipe out my family savings.

Regardless of what business school I attend, I'm certain that I want to attend class fulltime.

I could certainly go after an MBA the same way I secured my graduate engineering degree, but working while shuttling back and forth between Poughkeepsie and NYU in Manhattan was easily one of the most grueling ordeals I've ever put myself through.

Along with me being unemployed, my family will also have to relocate for me to get an MBA. Possibly as far away as California if I wind up at Stanford. There will definitely be some discomfort and inconvenience within the Brown household if we're all uprooted due to my MBA quest, but I tell myself that everyone will benefit once I'm successful. Still, I'm aware that there's an element of selfishness to my plan, which causes me to feel occasional tinges of guilt.

There's another factor behind my desire to make more money at IBM. Namely, in the last three years I've morphed from a slide rule-toting techie into a bona fide financial animal.

In a way this makes perfect sense, because to excel in either realm you've got to have a head for numbers, discipline, a bit of a perfectionist streak, and an ability to plan in a forward-looking way.

Thanks to having a family budget we never deviate from, and thanks to adhering to a fairly frugal lifestyle, Sylvia and I have had a little disposable income to work with the last few years. That led to a discussion about using investing as a vehicle to financial independence.

I've never been much of a reader of general interest materials, but I'm reading everything I can get my hands on about finance, investing, and the stock market. The other thing I'm addicted to is stories about successful people. I firmly believe that by studying their behaviors and habits, it's possible to glean things that will allow me to replicate their achievements.

At this point in my life I define success as having enough capital to make a significant splash in the world of charity. Success is having excess funds that will make it possible for Sylvia and I to travel and never have to worry about living paycheck to paycheck.

Those are fairly modest objectives, to be sure, but I'm only 28 and have never really had a chance to come face to face with true affluence, beyond what I've read in books and magazines. I do know that my present financial circumstances, which most people would likely consider cushy, are not enough for me.

This is hardly surprising from someone who started sauntering around Apopka, Florida, with a $1,000 bill in his pocket when he was nine. Uncle Jake was subtly programming me and now his spadework is starting to blossom.

Both Uncle Jake and Granddad were big on real estate, and fortunately the property-ownership gene was passed to me, too. When I moved to Poughkeepsie I initially rented a two-bedroom apartment, but it wasn't long before Sylvia and I bought a reasonably priced rental property, a little duplex.

We manage our income-producing acquisition jointly and fortunately it's in good shape, so we don't have to field a lot of calls from tenants. It's in a blue-collar section of town, but hardly what you would call a slum. Neither Sylvia nor I want to make a penny off anyone's misery. In fact, my original plan was for my family and I to move into a unit of the duplex after our two-year apartment lease expired.

But the duplex does such a good job of generating money above and beyond its expenses that I let it remain an income producer. So my wife and I purchase our first house, a modest four-bedroom Cape Cod with a fairly big front yard and a detached garage. I'm quite proud of myself for having made the transition to homeowner, but not because it represents some picket-fence, American-Dream ideal.

No, I had read somewhere that it is possible to generate personal capital through prudent leverage, and that one of the best ways to do that is through real estate. That's because you put in 10 percent of your own money, while borrowing 90 percent.

I'm starting to see that every penny I spend, every investment I make, every interest rate I embrace or reject is all part of an interconnected jigsaw puzzle that could yield financial freedom down the road if I play my cards correctly. It's a tremendously empowering, exciting way to view my young family's finances. Instead of feeling like a leaf in the wind, I'm firmly in control of my fiscal destiny.

But more than that, I'm pleasantly surprised to find that I love economics and finance. Dealing with numbers and predicting and manipulating financial outcomes is hugely gratifying.

IBM has unwittingly stoked my fire with a stock purchase plan that allows me to buy Big Blue stock at a 15 percent discount, and then have the purchase automatically deducted from my paycheck. This is turn has gotten me even more interested in the stock market, and I've assembled a marketable securities portfolio that's performing quite impressively from an earnings standpoint.

Basically I'm doing a lot of reading about how the stock market operates, and a lot of my investments are focused on technically oriented companies, since that's what I know best. I'm developing a knack, a sixth sense, for finding companies that wind up generating robust sales and earnings. Incredibly, I'm not getting corporate information by reading prospectuses or anything along those lines. Magazine and newspaper articles provide much of the background I use to make my stock-picking decisions. I lack the savvy to adroitly analyze financial statements, because I've never had any formal financial training.

Yet another reason I want to throw every ounce of my focus and energy into earning an MBA on a fulltime basis.

★   ★   ★

One night after Sylvia and I have eaten dinner and Tonya has been tucked into bed, Sylvia and I are happily lolling on the couch in the living room of our home, enjoying a rare moment of husband/wife relaxation on a work night. My spouse is in a pretty decent mood and has her legs casually draped over mine, so I take a deep breath and delve into a topic I've been waiting months to broach.

"It would be *awesome* if we could be the masters of our financial fate," I state casually, studying Sylvia's face. Apparently I've unwittingly said something quite humorous, because my better half is chuckling easily and playfully punches my arm.

"Okay, Eddie—what?" Sylvia asks, laughing. "I forgot to enter a check, right? Do I need to balance the checkbook?"

I sure hope she has that pretty smile on her face 10 minutes from now. I kinda doubt it.

"No, no," I respond, smiling myself. "Everything is fine, things are good. Our finances are in pretty good shape, but I know how they could be much better."

Sylvia's smile vanishes. "You're thinking about buying another rental property?"

"In the future, maybe. But not now. I was thinking of getting an MBA."

Frowning, Sylvia swings her legs from my lap to the floor. She was a good soldier when I got my master's in engineering from NYU, taking care of Tonya during my classes and giving me space when I needed to study during weekends and after coming home from IBM. She supported me without complaint during my NYU days, but at times there was definitely an underlying tension that we both glossed over.

"So you're going to be commuting again?" she asks in a voice that has a slight edge that wasn't there a moment ago. "And why do you need an MBA? You just got your engineering master's two years ago."

"Sweetie, I need an MBA so I can become a manager at IBM. Leading to even better benefits, and more money for the family." One of Sylvia's characteristics is that you never have to guess where you stand with her. She has a very demonstrative personality. It's clear from her frown and crossed arms that my sales pitch isn't going over well. Not at all.

"We're already doing okay now," Sylvia says, which I can't deny. "We've got a house, two cars, and a duplex that's making us money. You're making money from your stocks and we have money in the bank."

"That's all true," I reply. "But I—we—can do so much better. I can get us to a point where we don't have any financial worries. Where we can help poor college students get through school and not even miss the money we donate."

"So you're thinking about commuting again?"

"No. For me to get the most out of an MBA program, I think it would be best if I went fulltime."

"What?"

My wife is slow to anger, but on those rare occasions when her temper fully erupts, it's never pretty. Judging from the way Sylvia asked that last question, it's clear that she's ticked. I'm a little annoyed myself—that she doesn't instantly grasp how an MBA will create a rising tide that will lift all boats in the Brown household. There are a million potential impediments on the road to wealth generation, and I would really appreciate it if my spouse didn't turn out to be one of them.

"I think it would be a good idea to be a fulltime student. To make the best of the MBA classes I'll need to take, I'll need to fully immerse myself. And I was thinking that if I'm going to do this, why not go to one of the best MBA programs in the country?"

Sylvia rolls her eyes and sighs loudly. I hate it when she does that, which she's well aware of. This is going to be a full-fledged fight.

"So you're thinking about quitting work AND possibly moving?" she asks, her voice rising. "This seems far-fetched to me, Eddie. We live in a nice community, and we have really nice friends. And Tonya's doing well in the day care center we have her in. Have you considered all of these things?"

We go back and forth for a few more minutes about my MBA quest, with neither side backing down an inch, before Sylvia abruptly rises to get ready for bed, leaving me on the couch by myself. Thoroughly frustrated, I close my eyes and slowly collapse back against the sofa.

God, please help Sylvia get a long-term perspective on this MBA business. And please let me be making the right decision.

I rise from the couch and putter around in the kitchen for a few moments, before heading off to a bedroom that I know will make the North Pole seem like Miami. Oh well. I can't back down on this one, because I'm one hundred percent right . . . I think.

Unfortunately, Sylvia and I have another heated discussion about my MBA designs the following day, as well as the day after that. I am seeing a side of my wife I've never witnessed before—she's a tigress when it comes to shielding our family—especially Tonya—from anything that might adversely affect our stability.

My mate has labeled my desire to attend business school self-centered, which stings me tremendously because there's a kernel of truth there. After all, I'm the one who finds the process of identifying and purchasing successful technology stocks to be more fun than work. And I'm the one who's looking to trade in engineering for the more gratifying, and lucrative, field of finance, not Sylvia or Tonya.

But I still maintain that if I'm able to further hone my business and financial skills, my entire family will benefit, not just me. So I stick to my guns.

After four or five days of acrimony, Sylvia finally relents. In a manner that's grudging and that also makes it clear that she's still very, very angry with me, my spouse accedes to my desire to get an MBA. What should have been a very happy moment for me was instead bittersweet. I had always envisioned business training as enabling me to strengthen my family's financial standing, but all my ambition has done thus far is instigate an unprecedented level of marital strife before I've even taken a single class.

Capitalizing on my hard-won green light from Sylvia, I fill out what feels like a thousand-page application to the Consortium for Graduate Study in Business for Negroes. Part of the application process calls for me to write several essays, something I would ordinarily ask

Sylvia to help me with. Right now, however, there's an off chance that she might pull out a sword if I solicit her assistance, so I muddle through the essay writing alone.

Meanwhile, another crisis of sorts is playing out within my family. Like her father, Tonya began walking and talking before she was one and is a very verbal and confidant two year old. But for some reason, all the beautifully formed, self-assured sentences that made my chest burst with pride have mysteriously dried up and Tonya is now stuttering.

Sylvia thinks there may be something wrong with our baby's vocal cords. Personally, I have no idea what's afoot and am hoping it's just a phase that will go away after a few weeks or months. I do know that it's very disconcerting to hear Tonya stutter, and I always catch myself trying to will the thoughts and words out of my beautiful daughter's mouth. Whatever her malady is, it's added another layer of tension to an already tense household.

Following a month-long wait that feels like years, the Consortium finally responds to my application. I've been accepted! I briefly contemplate asking the Consortium people if they have someone who can convey the news to my bride, while I cower in one of those concrete Civil Defense atomic bomb shelters that were commonplace during the 1950s and 1960s.

But since the bad news is of my making, I might as well be its bearer. Sylvia seems genuinely happy for me when I tell her the Consortium has taken me into its ranks, and gives me a hug and a kiss. She's basically a kind and selfless person and clearly realizes what getting an MBA degree means to me. And of course I take pains to emphasize repeatedly—like about three million times—that all of my educational expenses are being subsidized, plus I get a living stipend.

I trust that eventually she'll come to appreciate how much this degree will mean to us, not just her husband.

With the Consortium's acceptance firmly in hand, I continue to agonize over whether I should take a run at Wharton, Harvard, and Stanford. Those first two choices are Ivy League, and I have to confess that the prospect of getting a degree from an Ivy League school fascinates me.

The first reason is practical—the Ivy League schools have many highly placed executives sprinkled throughout America's top corporations. I already know that Ivy Leaguers look out for each other from having observed the practice in action at IBM. They have a close-knit network of movers and shakers.

The second factor is strictly prestige. When you flash an MBA from Harvard or the Wharton School, there's just an automatic assumption that you're incredibly bright and competent, the crème de la crème. What this says about my personality I'm not sure, but I want to see those looks of awe and envy when people discover I'm an Ivy Leaguer.

However when I crunch the numbers on the Wharton School and Harvard, as well as Stanford, it just doesn't make economic sense to me. All of my expenses will be taken care of if I remain with the Consortium, and I seriously doubt that another Lady B. will magically appear and subsidize my expenses for those first three schools.

So I opt to stay with the Consortium for Graduate Study in Business for Negroes, which is headquartered at Washington University in St. Louis. The Consortium even takes care of tendering my application to Washington U's business school, along with Indiana's and Wisconsin's. If I'm accepted by all three, I get to list my first, second, and third preferences.

As it turns out, all three business schools associated with the Consortium admit me into their programs. Of the trio I happen to think Indiana is the best and rate it No. 1. So it appears that Sylvia, Tonya, and I will be moving to Bloomington, Indiana, to live for the next two years.

Prior to Bloomington, though, we'll be stopping in St. Louis for nine weeks. The Consortium for Graduate Study in Business for Negroes wants me and my classmates to take business classes at Washington University to make sure we're up to snuff before our MBA programs start.

This means Sylvia and I will need to put the lion's share of our household belongings in storage before heading off to St. Louis for the summer.

I have a realtor place our Poughkeepsie house on the market and to my everlasting relief our abode is snapped up fairly quickly. It would have been an absolute fiasco to have it sitting unsold while I'm off in St. Louis, taking Consortium classes, because that would have helped justify a certain person's reluctance for us to move. We actually make a little money off the sale, but Sylvia couldn't care less about that. An undisturbed nest is what she craves at the moment, along with a husband who won't turn things upside down at a moment's notice.

Once our Cape Cod sale goes through, only formalities remain—disconnect the utilities, sell one of our two cars, say goodbye to dear friends. That last thing is a particularly painful aspect of this move for Sylvia, and I hate having to watch her sever treasured relationships.

She'll build new friendships in Bloomington, Indiana, but it will take time. I'm not totally stupid—I'm aware of what she's going through. While she's making new friends, in the meantime all she'll have to fall back on is a frayed, quasi-contentious relationship with me.

When moving day finally arrives, I rent a U-Haul trailer and hitch it to a Chevrolet sedan that will serve as our only car for the foreseeable future. After cramming the U-Haul full of clothes and cooking utensils, I set off for St. Louis accompanied by an amiable, but still somewhat ticked off, spouse and a stuttering two-year-old.

All I can think about as we hit the interstate and head west is that I have no choice but to make this MBA I'm chasing pay off spectacularly once it's in my hands.

Chapter 9

A Famished Lion in a Butcher Shop

Who knew that Midwest heat and humidity could be every bit as oppressive as the weather back East? It's a brutally hot St. Louis day as my family and I drive onto the campus of Washington University, dragging our U-Haul trailer behind us. The three of us will be living in on-campus housing, so the first order of business is to get my ladies comfortably situated.

Washington University has an expansive, beautiful urban campus with plenty of grass and trees and one of the most impressive quadrangles I've ever laid eyes on. Physically it reminds me of Howard University, where I spent my undergrad days. As I run around the campus, looking for the area where my family's belongings will be stored over the next nine weeks, I feel a sense of excitement wash over me.

First of all because academic settings, and especially places of higher learning, always give me an anticipatory tingle. I love learning!

But I'm also kind of pleased with myself. Not many people would have left a comfortable engineering job at IBM to pursue an MBA, and they certainly wouldn't have uprooted their families to do so. But I did, and I can't help but think about Grandma and Uncle Jake as I take in Washington U's campus. The two of them always hammered into me that striving to optimize my chances for success was something I should always do.

They almost made it seem like accomplishment and prosperity was my manifest destiny. While I don't feel quite that strongly, I do feel that I have a bright future as long as I keep making an effort to hone and expand my skill set.

Once classes get underway, it's refreshing to encounter 35 other new members of the Consortium for Graduate Study in Business for Negroes who possess outlooks on life that are remarkably similar to mine. We're from various backgrounds and walks of life and are uniformly capable, ambitious, and serious-minded. We exude confidence and are interested in banding together to prove an essential point—we can all excel and achieve. Our collective mindset is that we're ready to run the entire world, not just the world of business, should the slightest opportunity to do so present itself.

It's clear that a stringent, uncompromising vetting process has been at play, because the Consortium Class of 1970 doesn't contain a single slacker, screw-off, or dreamer, just 36 feisty, highly focused students ready to kick butt and take names.

By the way, did I mention that we absolutely detest our organization's name? At a time when black pride is at its zenith, the "Negroes" part of the Consortium for Graduate Study in Business for Negroes makes our skin crawl. To offer an example of the tenor of the times, in a few weeks African-American Olympians Tommie Smith and John Carlos will be accepting their Olympic medals in Mexico City brandishing Black Power salutes.

Obviously my Consortium colleagues and I can't embrace that degree of radicalism if we're to have a prayer of successfully infiltrating the conservative executive suites of Corporate America, but the word Negroes seems far too antiquated for these times. My classmates and I let the folks running the Consortium know that Negroes is a demeaning term that needs to be changed to Blacks. The offending appellation remains while we're in the program, but sure enough Negroes is dropped before the Consortium Class of 1971 rolls through.

After a week or so of taking classes at Washington University, it's obvious that the curriculum is frustratingly remedial. A lot of us who feel we're ready for the big time rebel at the thought of participating in a basic program, including yours truly.

The Class of 1970 starts grousing about its desire to tackle coursework that isn't rudimentary in nature, although I think that on a certain level we all understand what's going on here. Namely, the inaugural class before us only had about 12 students, and anywhere from a third to one half of them washed out of the program. So the Consortium wants to make sure that my classmates and I are up to snuff academically. There's a major difference between us and our predecessors: most of the Class of 1969 came to the program directly from various undergraduate settings and lacked our work experience and maturity.

After the powers that be have a chance to observe my class's unwavering focus and strong academic performance, the nine-week remedial program gets scrapped for subsequent classes. In the end, I don't learn an awful lot from an academic standpoint during my nine weeks at Washington University. What I do learn is that it's possible for a bunch of highly accomplished alpha males, my Consortium comrades, to take their egos out of the equation and come together harmoniously in pursuit of a common goal. Top to bottom, it's the most impressive group I've had the privilege of joining, bar none.

A number of us are married and we and our spouses sometimes get together for dinner and other activities, which works out well for Sylvia after an entire day of interacting with our rambunctious two-year-old.

Another thing I learn during those sweltering nine weeks in St. Louis is that I married a tremendous woman who will go to extraordinary lengths to help her man get ahead in the world. And I come to appreciate that we have a tremendously resilient union that can probably withstand anything.

About halfway through the summer program at Washington University, I receive a flabbergasting phone call at my apartment one morning. I'm informed that IBM is going to pay 40 percent of my salary while I earn my MBA. I'll be doing this under the auspices of a very competitive technology program that annually involves only 20 of IBM's 250,000 employees.

Here's the gist of my unexpected IBM windfall: I have been placed in a highly sought-after program for employees seeking technology-related Ph.D. degrees. Under the terms of the program, I'm still considered a regular employee and my tenure will continue uninterrupted. Plus I get to keep all my benefits, including health insurance, in addition to 40 percent of my regular compensation. IBM will also pay for temporary housing and for moving my family's belongings. For a fleeting second I wonder if one of my IBM colleagues is playing a practical joke on me.

The IBM executive who's contacted me, the manager of education at the Poughkeepsie facility where I worked, stops talking and awaits my response. Hearing stunned silence, he asks how the IBM program sounds to me? To which I offer the following response: "Wow!"

Naturally I'm curious as heck to know how I came to be a beneficiary of this surprise corporate largesse. When I ask how things unfolded, I'm told it was a managerial decision.

But I'm going after an MBA, so how do I fit into a program for Ph.D. candidates? Who in management made that decision? And what motivated them to do it?

I keep all those wonderful questions to myself, where they belong. I've examined this gift horse about as thoroughly as I dare.

When I hang up the phone, I'm laughing in disbelief.

"Oh man! Oh man!"

Sylvia comes sauntering in from another room of our small on-campus apartment, where she was putting Tonya down for a nap.

"What, Eddie? What's so funny?"

I inform her of our stroke of good fortune, then get a pencil and a piece of paper and start doing some budgetary math. I look at the paper and start laughing again. Based on my calculations, my family and I are going to have more disposable after-tax income than we had when I was back in Poughkeepsie.

Even Sylvia is impressed when I inform her of this, and she looks rather relieved, too. Given that she's not working—I didn't dare ask her to come along on this MBA odyssey AND work—it appeared that we were going to be working with a very tight budget during my two years in business school.

IBM has just put us on easy street. My wife wisecracks that the three of us are gypsies living out of our car and U-Haul trailers, but at least now we won't be gypsies who've taken a vow of poverty.

With me usually occupied with business school duties, Sylvia spends the bulk of her time in our small apartment with Tonya. Our new digs are a far cry from the bucolic home we left in Poughkeepsie, and I'm impressed by how my wife isn't complaining and is going out of her way to be supportive. However, I've known her long enough to appreciate I'm not totally out of the doghouse yet. That's fair, because she is making a tremendous sacrifice for what was essentially a unilateral decision on my part.

Aside from this whole MBA thing, another stressor in my marriage is Tonya's continued stuttering. Instead of getting better, it seems to be getting worse by the day.

Before we rent another U-Haul trailer and drive off to Bloomington, Indiana, and the campus of Indiana University, my wife and I agree that if Tonya's condition doesn't get better soon, one of our first priorities will be to find Bloomington's best speech therapist.

★ ★ ★

Thankfully, the move from St. Louis to Bloomington was considerably shorter than the one from Poughkeepsie to St. Louis. I'm back in small-town America again, in a town whose fortunes wax and wane based on what's happening with its biggest employer, Indiana University.

The school has a humongous campus, much bigger than those of Washington or Howard. Sylvia and I get a nice little apartment that's literally on-campus, allowing me to walk to class. My proximity proves a godsend when I have to trek to and from class when it's snowing. Another nice thing about our apartment is that the nursery school we use is directly next to our apartment building, making Sylvia's life easier.

When the first day of class arrives, I feel a familiar tingle of excitement. Whenever I enter a learning environment, I feel like a famished lion wandering into a butcher shop!

There's just something thrilling about being in an environment where everything is knowledge-based, and where my primary responsibility is to cram as much information as I possibly can into my head. I'm here to learn as much as I can about business—I'm here to be an educational glutton.

Further fueling my excitement at Indiana is a cadre of eleven brilliant, resolute young black men who also belong to Indiana's 1970 MBA class. My Consortium buddies and I, or the "Special Twelve" as we call ourselves, are practically the only blacks in the business school. Their camaraderie and encouragement make the task of earning an MBA degree easier.

Twelve other Consortium members went to the University of Wisconsin, while 12 more stayed in St. Louis and are taking the MBA classes at Washington University.

At Indiana, I find some of the most fascinating courses to be finance, marketing, and organizational behavior. I'm surprised at my fondness for those last two, because I've always gravitated toward quantitative coursework. During my undergraduate days, I would have scoffed at marketing and organizational behavior as soft classes, because of their focus on immeasurable things like attitudes and feelings. Thanks to maturation, I understand how key it is to understand the human side of capitalism. Indiana's MBA curriculum is giving me a far more holistic approach to business. Getting a company to optimize its performance always entails more than simply getting metrics to align favorably. You also have to deftly manage human dynamics that affect customers and employees.

In the meantime, I'm getting one other critically important lesson on human interactions and their ramifications. This isn't in a classroom, though, but it's inside my own home.

As I mentioned, Sylvia and I had pledged to get professional help for Tonya if her stuttering didn't improve. It hasn't in the time we've been in Bloomington, so my wife and I track down a speech therapist that we feel comfortable with and start taking Tonya to her office. Sylvia is insistent that something must be wrong with our child's vocal cords. Personally, I'm not going to hazard a guess.

I can speak knowledgeably about electronic circuits and transistors and even capital budgeting, but I have no clue why my beautiful daughter's words always seem to catch agonizingly in her throat.

I just know that I hope it stops, and soon.

After having Tonya submit to physical tests that thankfully fail to reveal any problems, the speech therapist starts asking Sylvia and I questions. Stuff about our usual routine, how we run our household, and even what kind of foods we eat.

After about four visits, the speech therapist lays a diagnosis on Sylvia and I that floors us—Tonya is stuttering because of our parenting! Specifically, all of the bickering and tension associated with my decision to stop working at IBM and get an MBA. If my wife and I talk over our differences more calmly, and never in front of Tonya, odds are that her stuttering will disappear, the therapist informs us. I look over at Sylvia and her expression is every bit as pained as mine is. We have no clue whether the therapist knows what she's talking about, but just the thought that we might have caused emotional turmoil for Tonya is tremendously hurtful.

My disbelief quickly gives way to a sense of guilt that keeps me from making eye contact with my wife or the speech therapist. Or Tonya. None of them precipitated the MBA angst that rocked the Brown family—I did.

Even though it probably wasn't her intention, I feel as though the speech therapist is implicitly blaming me for the drama that's been swirling through my household for about the last three months. My face is burning with embarrassment as I look at Tonya, who's off to the side and innocently playing with brightly colored toys on the floor as Sylvia and I sit in front of the therapist's desk.

Chastened, I leave the office and resolve to never bicker with my wife in front of Tonya again. Sure enough, after a couple of months Tonya's stuttering stops and she's back to expressing her thoughts in beautifully worded, full sentences. Sylvia and I have gained a valuable bit of information about the dos and don'ts of parenting, and we've learned it the hard way.

I'm also getting a valuable lesson about being married to the former Sylvia Thurston. Namely, when she objects to something because she thinks it may not be in our family's best interest, in the future it might be a good idea to heed her objections. Unless I'm going after something with life-or-death ramifications, it's probably wiser to simply give in and maintain the peace in Chez Brown.

Out of the blue one day, Sylvia suggests that since we're living within a stone's throw of Indiana University, maybe she could get a master's in health education. Allowing us to kill two educational birds with one stone? I can't agree to this suggestion fast enough.

Because I'm making more now on an after-tax basis than I did in Poughkeepsie, Sylvia and I are able to pay for her classes out of our pockets.

While she studies health education, I'm totally immersing myself into the graduate business curriculum. With each passing semester I can feel my sophistication growing in terms of how I look at businesses and assess them. The satisfaction I gain from this is akin to someone who's been diligently working out in the gym and is finally starting to see well-defined biceps and deltoids.

The muscles I'm building aren't visible, but they get stronger every time I go to class, and will eventually enable me to build impressive wealth and support robust philanthropy. I'm doing mental isometrics that hopefully in a decade or so will yield a fat wallet.

If I sound very narrowly focused and mercenary, believe me when I tell you that every one of my MBA classmates, including the Special Twelve, are unabashedly striving for the same thing. It's possible to ascribe one's entry into medical school, or even law school, purely to altruism, but you'll never hear that from business school types.

Yes, replicating Lady B.'s generosity is a motivator for me, but so is getting Sylvia, Tonya, and I to eventually lead lives free of monetary worries. Ninety-nine percent of U.S. citizens want the same thing, but MBA students tend to be more upfront than most when it comes to admitting it.

Indiana University's business school is giving me valuable insights into how businesses are run and what constitutes good management. I'm also cobbling together an analytical framework for making considered judgments about public companies, as well as privately-held ones.

MBA coursework is so much fun that the prospect of my first year eventually coming to a close almost makes me feel sad. Fortunately before that takes place I get some wonderful news in the middle of my spring semester, in the form of a phone call from a top IBM executive that I've come to view as my mentor, Lars Anabuski.

Lars, who heads a key marketing group for IBM, is curious if I would like to come to IBM's marketing division in White Plains, New York, to do some marketing work over the summer. This would be undertaken at the same salary I was being paid when I left IBM.

I'm a little skeptical about IBM's marketing division, because it seems to me that the people there practice a black art that doesn't produce tangible goods or services, but that sucks budgetary dollars away from those who do. I still have a little of my if you can't quantify it, it's not real bias.

However, I also have a household to support and no summer employment prospects that will pay me anywhere near what I'll make back at White Plains. Plus I feel indebted to Lars, because I strongly suspect that he was the one who engineered my inclusion in an IBM program geared toward technology Ph.D. candidates.

Also, Sylvia and I are expecting another child! So it's basically a no-brainer to take Lars up on his offer.

After ending my first year at Indiana University with grades that put me in the top quarter of my MBA class, my family and I head back East. Yep, once again a U-Haul trailer shadows our car, now a Mercury Cougar, halfway across the country. I might add that it's a Cougar containing a hyperactive toddler who's bouncing off the walls and a pregnant spouse who keeps likening our situation to that of the Beverly Hillbillies.

I'm not sure if that comment is being uttered totally in jest, but I guess I have it coming. Of course the minute she takes her shoes off in the car, I zing her about returning to New York State barefoot and pregnant.

After getting my family settled in a Yonkers, New York, apartment, I spend the summer working at IBM's marketing division headquarters in White Plains, where I tackle projects forwarded to me by Lars. While I'm grateful to him, my suspicion that marketing probably isn't my cup of tea is confirmed. For one thing, it's a little too amorphous, too fuzzy, for my tastes. For another, I like work where the end result is concrete, and where there's a clear link to your efforts. That's not an indictment of marketing, but just stems from the way my brain is hardwired.

During my summer stint at IBM my second daughter, Jennifer, arrives on the scene. So, I head back to Indiana University for the second year of my MBA coursework with a trailer attached to a Mercury Cougar that now contains a squalling newborn and a very active three-year-old. You haven't lived until you try that at least once.

Chapter 10

The Height of Duplicity and Betrayal?

Next to nepotism, mentorship and networking are the most powerful forces that can impact a businessperson's career. I'm about to discover that shortly, thanks to my association with Indiana University (IU).

I'm presently on the verge of wrapping up my MBA studies and am really looking forward to returning to IBM as a manager. Frankly, I marvel at the transformation I've undergone at IU, compared to when I first set foot on the school's campus two years ago.

Back then I had a pretty good intuitive sense of how the worlds of economics, finance, and management are interwoven. But in the time that's elapsed since those early days, my grasp of business has expanded exponentially. My newfound expertise and the chutzpah of youth make me feel as though I could slide into the CEO's office when I return to IBM!

As far as I'm concerned, if you go through an MBA program that doesn't make you feel that way, you haven't gone through a good one. My instruction at Indiana has been uniformly excellent, and my performance has risen to the occasion.

Word has reached a former IU classmate, a gentleman named Clarence Malone, that I'm something of a business school hotshot. An older, distinguished black man who isn't associated with the Consortium, Clarence has taken a position with a concern in Columbus, Indiana, known as Irwin Management Co., after getting his MBA from Indiana.

I'd met Clarence during my first year at IU and was immediately impressed by his worldliness and overall gravitas. Some people just have an aura that automatically makes you take them seriously, and Clarence is one of them.

Toward the end of my last semester at Indiana University, I get a call from Clarence, who kindly tells me that he's sung my praises at Irwin Management, and I can expect a call from one of their top executives.

Bear in mind that I have no desire to go anywhere after graduation other than IBM, plus I have no idea what kind of financial work Clarence is doing at Irwin. Nor do I know what Irwin does, for that matter. But I have a world of respect for Clarence and I figure it can't hurt to listen, so I thank him for his glowing recommendation and await a call from Irwin.

It comes the following day, and it's from a vice president named Harold Higgins. He's suggesting that he drive 35 miles from Columbus, Indiana, so that we can meet for dinner. "Am I okay with that?"

Sure. Why wouldn't I be? Not only do I have nothing to lose, but it's flattering to be subjected to a corporate full-court press prior to even earning my MBA. So one night after class I hook up with Higgins in one of Bloomington's nicer restaurants.

A handsome man whose hair is completely gray, Higgins is exceedingly polished and thoughtful and is wearing what appears to be a dark Brooks Brothers suit. In addition to being one of those listeners who makes you feel like the most captivating speaker in the world, Higgins is also a gifted raconteur. Over dinner he spins a marvelous tale that's the most riveting business story I've ever heard, far better than the case studies I've been perusing for class.

It's the tale of how Irwin Management came to be.

Basically, Irwin Management's raison d'etre is to serve as a private investment firm for the richest family in Indiana, which is based in Columbus. Higgins traces the family's staggering wealth back to what's easily one of the more prescient allocations of seed capital in the history of free enterprise. Seems that in the 1910s, a noted Columbus banker, investor, and real estate maven named W.G. Irwin helped self-taught local mechanic and inventor Clessie Cummins get the Cummins Engine Co., off the ground. Cummins, who served as the Irwin family's chauffeur, was convinced that the new diesel technology he was tinkering with would wind up having tremendous utility, so he spent countless hours working on diesel engines and improving them.

If you've ever heard of the Cummins Diesel Company, or used one of their products, you've got Clessie Cummins to thank for that. Along with Irwin, who provided financial support for 17 years as Cummins sought to perfect the diesel engine.

In the 1930's W.G. Irwin's great nephew, Joseph Irwin Miller, became the general manager of Cummins Engine, and turned it into an international powerhouse in the diesel engine industry. A naval officer during World War II and a Phi Beta Kappa graduate of Yale University, where he majored in Greek and Latin, J. Irwin Miller is the patriarch of the family currently being served by Irwin Management Co. The main drivers behind the Miller family's nonstop wealth creation are Cummins Engine, along with Irwin Union Bank & Trust, the largest bank in southern Indiana.

As Higgins weaves his tale, I make a conscious effort not to go slack-jawed. The thought of a Fortune 500 company *and* a prosperous bank working around the clock to create wealth for one family is a mindboggling concept to this 29 year old from Apopka, Florida. Sure beats the heck out of having a handful of rental properties and a modest investment portfolio in your corner. I'm instantly intrigued.

Higgins has undoubtedly noted this, because he's been studying me very closely. Even though he's a model of subtlety, I sense that he's been mentally poking, prodding, and assessing me the entire time we've been together. But the beauty of participating in an interview like this one is, I didn't request it. So there's zero pressure. Reasonably certain that I have a bright future with IBM, a Fortune

100 multinational, I'm perfectly relaxed as Higgins smoothly takes a sip of wine and resumes his story.

Irwin Management Co., he tells me, has a team of 85 people to oversee the vast financial fortune of J. Irwin Miller, his wife, their five children, a sister, and Miller's aunt. Irwin Management has a marketable securities group whose main area of focus is investing Miller assets. In Houston, Irwin Management maintains a small office for an oil and gas group concentrating on investment opportunities in those two areas.

There's also a real estate group that pursues national real estate interests for the Miller family, as well as a consulting group whose sole purpose is to prepare J. Irwin Miller for the meetings of outside boards of directors he belongs to.

Of Irwin Management's 85-member staff, 45 hold MBAs. Everyone with an MBA degree, Higgins mentions offhandedly, was one of the top three students in their business school classes and have earned their degrees at Harvard, Stanford, and the Wharton Business School. Irwin Management also has lawyers, CPAs, and a private chef who cooks for the management firm's special guests!

Now I'm the one who's closely scrutinizing Higgins as I try to determine if he's pulling my leg. There's a family so fabulously rich that it employs 85 people for the sole purpose of perpetuating the clan's wealth? Is this a gambit on Higgins' part to see if I'm the gullible type? A joke? Over the course of a two-hour introductory dinner, Higgins has blown away my definition of what it means to be wealthy.

Even so, I'm sitting in the restaurant with what I hope is an unimpressed look on my face, as though I routinely hang out with people as wealthy as the Miller family. And in all honesty, there's a side of me that's not impressed. J. Irwin Miller may be worth the gross national product of a small country, but that doesn't mean squat to me if he's not philanthropic. I have yet to hear one word about how, or if, he uses his power and influence to assist those less fortunate.

Dabbing my mouth with a fancy white linen napkin following an excellent meal of grouper, I lean forward slightly. Higgins' response to my next question is of paramount importance to me.

"J. Irwin Miller and Irwin Management would seem well-positioned to make a huge impact on the world of philanthropy," I observe. "Is that a priority?"

"I think you could safely say that, Ed," Higgins responds with a light laugh. "Mr. Miller and his family have three separate foundations under the aegis of what's known as the Family of Foundations. For starters there's the Cummins Engine Foundation, which he founded in 1954. There's also a foundation that's been established by the family, and their bank operates a foundation, too.

"By the way, Cummins Engine was one of the first companies to promise to donate five percent of its net income to charity. Specifically, the Cummins Engine Foundation."

With that last observation from Higgins, my internal pendulum swings from mild interest in Irwin Management Co., to being totally impressed by the organization and everything it represents. It specializes in what motivated me to earn an MBA in the first place, wealth creation, and it appears to have a strong philanthropic presence and a social conscience.

Now I can't help but wonder what kind of role Higgins has envisioned for me within the exotic apparatus he works for, a kind of place I had no clue existed prior to dinner tonight. I know darn well he didn't travel 35 miles from Columbus to simply break bread and engage in casual chitchat.

"Is Mr. Miller politically active?" I ask Higgins. Miller's politics will tell me a lot about him, to possibly include why he and his firm might have an interest in me.

"Yes, you could safely say he has an interest in politics," Higgins responds. "Religion, too. Not only is he a power broker in the liberal wing of the Republican Party, but Mr. Miller helped establish the National Council of Churches back in 1950 and became its first lay president several years later.

"He chaired the NCC's Commission on Religion and Race, which was a sponsor of the March on Washington," Higgins adds, as if sensing the underlying reason for my question. "Mr. Miller also headed religious delegations that met with presidents Kennedy and Johnson to push for the Civil Rights Act of 1964.

"I could go on," Higgins says, giving our waiter a barely perceptible nod to bring our check, "but I'll end by telling you that three
years ago, Mr. Miller served as chairman for an American Medical
Association conference on health care for the poor."

I'm halfway tempted to jokingly ask if Miller walks on water, too,
but I think better of it. And I make no effort to disguise the fact that
I'm now thoroughly taken with J. Irwin Miller and Irwin Management.

My meal with the urbane Harold Higgins draws to a close, and
he notes with apparent sincerity that he enjoyed my company, as well
as our conversation. Before I leave, Higgins gives me a heads-up that
I can probably expect a phone call from Irwin Management Co., to
set up a second interview. If I'm interested, that is.

To my surprise I hear myself tell Higgins that, yes, I would definitely be interested in having a second meeting, and that I look
forward to hearing from him, or one of his representatives.

I have a commitment to fulfill with IBM—a debt of gratitude to
repay—so I don't know why I'm leading Higgins on like this.

As I drive back to my apartment afterward, I can't stop thinking
about the old axiom, the rich get richer. Why in the heck wouldn't
they, when they have entities like Irwin Management Co., diligently
looking for ways to make an already impressive status quo even rosier?

I wonder if Lady B. had anyone managing her wealth. I also
wonder if I'll ever reach a point where I'll need my own Irwin
Management Co., to tend to my family's interests.

After I return home and tell Sylvia about J. Irwin Miller and Irwin
Management Co., she's as wide-eyed as I was back in the restaurant.
It just boggles the mind to think that while we're here obediently
adhering to our very modest family budget, there are fabulously rich
families out there employing nearly 100 people in order to generate
even more family wealth.

I'm even a little chagrined and embarrassed that I find this so
astounding. I had fancied myself the consummate financial sophisticate
prior to dinner, when in reality I didn't know jack about how the top
one percent live. In my defense, if you've never been exposed to something, how could you conceivably expect to anticipate its existence?

I pride myself on having a personality that rarely swings to one
extreme or the other, but I am tremendously excited about my dinner

with Harold Higgins and about Irwin Management Co. If this isn't readily apparent to Sylvia the minute I walk through the door of our apartment, I'm sure there's little doubt in her mind after I talk her head off for the better part of an hour.

"Ed, this sounds like an interesting opportunity," she says at one point. "But what about IBM? Don't you have an obligation?"

I immediately feel a pang of guilt. Yeah, I do have an obligation to return to the world's largest computer manufacturer. My word is bond, so I don't know why I even agreed to accompany Higgins to dinner in the first place.

Yet, when his secretary calls the following day to arrange a meeting at Irwin Management's offices, I agree. About two weeks before my Indiana University coursework ends, I set out for Columbus, Indiana, to find out exactly what it is these Irwin Management people have in mind. I feel a bit like a kid who knows he's not supposed to raid the cookie jar but can't help himself, as I pull into Columbus, a town of roughly 26,000 people that's about 40 miles south of Indianapolis.

Surprisingly, Columbus has an extraordinary, memorable skyline for a town its size. Not in terms of hulking skyscrapers, but in terms of the architecture displayed by many of its buildings. I'm not an architecture devotee, per se, but it's apparent as soon as you enter Columbus that something extraordinary is afoot.

When I met with Harold Higgins, he told me how J. Irwin Miller struck a deal to have the Cummins Foundation pay the architect fees for new public buildings in Columbus. A renaissance man who's a patron of architecture, Miller arranged for some of the brightest luminaries in the world of architecture, to include Eero Saarinen, I.M. Pei, and Richard Meier, to design Columbus buildings ranging from libraries to shopping areas to churches to Miller's own home. *Smithsonian Magazine* has called Columbus "a veritable museum of modern architecture."

Even the untrained eye instantly hews to the bold and imaginative lines displayed by quite a few of Columbus' buildings, of which six are National Historic Landmarks. It's almost as though I've entered some kind of imaginary J. Irwin Miller fiefdom where he's managed to put his stamp all over his kingdom. As I drive toward Irwin

Management offices, there's one predominant thought in my head—I sure hope I get to meet this man.

I'm not granted an audience with Miller during my visit, although I am grilled by a number of Irwin Management executives. Again, I feel no pressure to speak of, because IBM is going to take me back into their fold. I know this for a fact because I've been talking with them regarding which part of the country I'd like to work in when I return. A tentative understanding has been reached that my next stop will be in Colorado.

But following my second interview at Irwin Management, it's clear to me that I find them more attractive than IBM. At International Business Machine, I'll be one of thousands of junior executives falling over themselves to chase the brass ring.

At Irwin Management, on the other hand, I'll be taught to manage money. I'll get a crash course on the generation and perpetuation of wealth, and in incredibly rarefied environment that most people don't even know exists.

I make a decision regarding Irwin Management with the same analytical, methodical approach that I use to make most major decisions—I just do it a lot faster than normal, because I'm practically at the end of my MBA coursework.

I want to work for Irwin. Period.

However, it's critically important for Sylvia and I to be on the same page regarding Irwin Management. Without her buy-in, I definitely won't accept any position Irwin offers. If Sylvia casts a dissenting vote, I'm prepared to take my family and head out west to Colorado and IBM once I earn my MBA.

As incredibly attractive as Irwin Management Co., is, it's not worth wrecking my family or marriage over. I learned my lesson when Tonya started stuttering after we left Poughkeepsie. Anyway, I kind of owe Sylvia one after she followed me to Indiana University.

Fortunately, the folks at Irwin Management make my sales job considerably easier by inviting my wife and I to dinner with some of the organization's top executives and their spouses.

The Irwin Management folks we dine with, and their spouses, couldn't be nicer or more down-to-earth. I feel at ease immediately, and so does Sylvia. Given that Tonya is about to enter first grade,

Sylvia quizzes the wives about schools in Columbus, while I ask the guys very general, open-ended questions. Despite their high-powered Ivy League credentials, they come across as a very congenial, modest bunch, and so do their wives.

The chemistry on all sides clicks. Sylvia and I drive back to Bloomington secure in the knowledge that we can do the Small Town America thing in Columbus—as well as get along with the Irwin Management crew.

After driving to Columbus for an additional interview, I still haven't laid eyes on J. Irwin Miller. However, Higgins finally shows his hand in terms of what Irwin Management has in mind for me. I'm offered the position of assistant to the president's office.

The assistant in the title makes the opportunity sound junior in nature, but in reality the job is an important one with a lot of responsibility, as well as clout. The position being offered to me was once held by the current president of Cummins Engine Co., Hank Schott. In fact, the last three assistants to the president's office at Irwin Management have segued into high-ranking executive positions at Cummins Engine. Having finally played his ace-in-the-hole card, Higgins stares at me, waiting for my answer.

"Harold, I'm flattered that you think that highly of me," I tell him as I sit in his office in front of his desk. "You run a first-rate organization here that employs some incredibly capable and bright individuals. I like being around smart people," I laugh. "I would love to work here, thank you."

Higgins comes from behind his desk and gives me a warm handshake.

"If anyone is flattered, it's Irwin Management," he says. "We would consider it a privilege to have the opportunity to work in concert with someone of your caliber!"

Harold Higgins always seems to have just the right words for any situation. Here I am two days away from earning my MBA, and he's making it seem as though I should tell him "you're welcome!" for offering me a job at Irwin Management.

"Harold, we can be totally upfront with each other, right?"

"That's the only way we know how to operate, Ed," he replies, still grasping my hand. "What's up?"

"I really don't have much interest in moving on to Cummins, even if it's in a senior management role. But what I would like to do eventually is become a part of the marketable securities group here."

Even though Higgins is a smooth operator, this last comment has caught him off guard and his face registers a look of surprise. I'm probably the first recruit who didn't salivate and turn back flips at the prospect of possibly becoming part of the Cummins Engine senior management team.

However, running a company has never been high on my wish list. Making lots and lots of money, on the other hand, is. That's been the case since the days when Lady B. made it possible for me to get through Howard University.

I think about that as I walk out of Higgins office, having just accepted an offer to join Irwin Management. After I reach my car in the parking lot, I just sit in it and reflect for a couple of seconds before turning the ignition. Basically, I'm already feeling incredibly conflicted.

That's because I consider myself honest and trustworthy and pretty much lacking in guile. But the simple fact is, I have a handshake agreement to come back and work for IBM once I have my MBA from Indiana University. IBM paid me 40 percent of my salary the entire time I was in business school, something the computer maker didn't have to do.

From a financial standpoint, my family and I have had a remarkably comfortable financial run while I've been at Indiana University, and I've got IBM to thank for that. They also kept my healthcare and retirement benefits current.

For me to accept a job with Irwin Management a few days prior to getting my MBA feels like the height of duplicity and betrayal. I've never done anything comparable to this in my life, and it doesn't sit well with me.

What am I going to do? Basically, I have no idea, but I spend a fitful night after accepting the Irwin Management offer. When I walk across the commencement stage to accept my MBA, I feel guilty instead of jubilant. I wonder if anyone in the audience can sense that I'm basically a well-educated corporate pickpocket, one who has fleeced one of the country's biggest companies?

I envy the other members of the Special Twelve, my Consortium classmates. My colleagues have all graduated, and their pride and joy in their achievement is unalloyed. I don't share my IBM dilemma with any of them for fear of ruining their days of days. And because I don't want them to think poorly of me after learning how I've hoodwinked IBM.

Another sleepless night comes following graduation, as well as the night after that. Sylvia says I should send a letter of explanation to the executives at IBM who kindly threw their support behind my MBA quest.

I'm not sure if a letter will do the trick, but it's clear that I need to resolve this uncomfortable situation one way or another. Soon, too, because I hate the way I'm feeling about myself right now.

Chapter 11

A Window on the Top 1 Percent

I firmly believe that by the time you get to be about 30, the contours of your personality are pretty well filled in. I also believe that whenever you deviate from who you are, that invariably brings intense personal discomfort and disorientation.

Over the course of 29 years I've been a straight arrow who immediately fesses up to mistakes and who goes out of his way to avoid even the semblance of dishonesty. So it's no wonder I can't sleep at night and have been feeling vaguely disgusted with myself the last few days—I'm living a horrible lie.

That's why I've asked Sylvia to keep Tonya out of the bedroom of our apartment, so I can make an important phone call. It's time to contact IBM and face the music.

The secretary of the IBM executive who's my mentor, Lars Anabuski, gets on the line. Instead of the clipped, businesslike tone I'm used to hearing, today Lars' secretary fills the phone with surprising warmth.

"Eddie, congratulations on your MBA," she says. "We're all very proud of you, and know you'll put your degree to good use."

Yes, I think, *it will be put to good use. Just not with IBM, unfortunately.*

There's a brief pause, then a voice I've been absolutely dreading comes on the line.

"How's IBM's next CEO doing?" Lars says jovially, his laughter booming in my ear. "I'm sure you were the top student in your class!"

"Not exactly, Lars," I reply in subdued tone. "But I've been in the top quarter of my class throughout. And I really appreciate all the support that you, and IBM, have given me."

On the other side of my locked bedroom door, I can hear Tonya laughing hysterically as she plays with Sylvia. I wish I were out there having fun with them. In fact, I'd rather be anywhere else—including at the dentist's office undergoing a root canal—than making this infernal phone call.

"Don't mention it, Eddie," Lars says. "It's in IBM's best interest to identify our next generation of leaders. Your performance and your character made it easy."

I feel like groaning. Not in the best frame of mind before picking up the phone, I feel lower than whale poop after Lars utters that last comment. His high praise is embarrassing enough, but did he have to throw in "character"? Hearing that word makes my heart sink.

"You and the family ready to head west to Colorado?" Lars asks.

"Well, actually I wanted to talk to you about that."

I had rehearsed in my head several times how this conversation would play out. But the butterflies in my stomach have sent my speech floating into the ether. Time to stop messing around and simply lay my cards on the table.

"Lars I really, really appreciate the company supporting me while I got my MBA," I say, figuring that it can't hurt to reiterate my gratitude. "But a very attractive opportunity has come along. Has there ever been a case where an employee chosen for this selective program didn't return?"

Lars remains silent for several agonizing seconds. "It's not common, Eddie, but it's happened before," he says slowly. "You don't want to come back?"

"No, no, it's not that at all. IBM has been a terrific place to work. I've worked with some very impressive people who've taught me a lot, including you. And I've been involved with some fascinating projects. But my long-term goal has always been to generate wealth—for my family and for philanthropy. I've been offered a job by an organization that manages the wealth of the richest family in Indiana. There's no position at IBM that will give me that kind of experience."

There! My dark secret is finally in the open and it feels damn good to be rid of it. I would only turn my back on IBM for a once-in-a-lifetime opportunity. And that's precisely what Irwin Management Co. is.

"Tell you what, Eddie," Lars says. "Number one, you're clearly passionate about this offer, whatever it is. I don't think a man should be held back from things that get his juices going. Number two, if your plan is not to return, the door will always be open for you here at IBM. And I do mean always."

Lars Anabuski and IBM have been a class act from the first day I walked through the door right up to this very moment. And if my aim in life was to be a well-compensated technocrat, I'd have to be a madman to leave. But I have no interest in continuing to make my living through an association with engineering and technology, unless it's to invest in companies specializing in those areas.

I've reinvented myself, as Lars himself acknowledges after I tell him about Irwin Management. When I hang up the phone, it is with a towering sense of relief that Lars was so gracious and understanding. I'm also relieved that the IBM phase of my life is officially coming to an end.

There's a jaunty spring in my step as I slide across the bedroom floor, unlock the door and open it. Sylvia looks up from the floor, where she and Tonya are working in a coloring book, and immediately springs to her feet.

"Well?" she asks, fully aware of the turmoil my IBM predicament has caused me over the last few days. In deference to Tonya's perceptive and highly sensitive personality, we've made it a point to only have our IBM/Irwin Management discussions while Tonya is at day care, or asleep.

"I told IBM," I inform my spouse. "Lars says he understands completely, gave me his blessings, and wishes the four of us much luck. Time for me to learn how to make us some real money!"

Sylvia pulls me tight against her soft body and kisses me on the lips. "No regrets?" she asks, smiling.

That's my cue to laughingly mangle one of 1969's biggest pop hits, "My Way," by Frank Sinatra. "Regrets, I've had a few, but then again, too few to mention—"

"Ed!"

"Yeah?"

"I'm so glad you make your living off your brain and not your vocal cords!" Sylvia notes playfully. "Let's get this place packed and head to Columbus."

Our on-campus digs at Indiana University are so small that we're packed in no time. Sylvia and I are highly motivated to leave, too, because our apartment has been a fairly tight fit for the two of us along with Tonya and Jennifer.

I promised Sylvia that I would buy our family a proper house in Columbus, and I waste little time following through on that pledge. Nothing fancy, just a basic home with both front and back yards that provides our little people room to stretch their legs. Making the transition from a college campus where we occasionally heard drunken revelers in the wee hours of the morning, to a real abode was fairly easy.

In fact that transition is easier than moving from a global corporate leviathan with hundreds of thousands of employees to a Columbus-based enterprise employing 85 workers. The headquarters of Irwin Management Co. are in a two-story brick building at the corner of 3rd and Washington streets in Columbus' business district, on the town's extreme southwestern edge.

An ornate white wooden façade supported by thin, stylish columns creates a porch-like area at Irwin Management's front door where people can knock snow from their boots or shake water from their umbrellas during inclement weather.

The employees of Irwin Management Co. are nice to a fault, even the Houston-based oil and gas crew that I've yet to meet face-to-face. Everyone is bending over backward to make me feel welcome. It just takes me a couple of days to adjust to Irwin Management's rhythms, its internal heartbeat, if you will.

The organization just approaches things differently than IBM. The pace at Irwin tends to be a little more leisurely, and the sense of urgency is turned down a couple of notches. Irwin Management lacks that hunter/gatherer electricity that always crackled through IBM.

That could be because the specter of restive, hard-to-please shareholders is nonexistent. Or it may be because the fortunes of J. Irwin Miller, and his family, were established decades ago, and what's called for now is contemplative, deliberative wealth stewardship and enhancement.

I just know that Irwin Management has the calmest, most serene work environment I've experienced. It's also the most cerebral corporate culture I've yet to encounter, because there are some pretty deep thinkers around here. In fact, it wouldn't surprise me at all if Irwin Management has a higher proportion of MENSA members than any place I've ever been in my life.

Not that I find this intimidating—actually, it's incredibly stimulating. Being around the best and the brightest makes me dig deep, and I like that.

As Irwin Management Co.'s newest assistant to the president's office, I get a small second-floor office and a secretary. I report to the wealth-management firm's president, George Newlin, as well as to Harold Higgins, who's the vice president. My focus is a steady stream of special projects and assignments that these two executives dole out to me.

My very first assignment puts me in tangential contact with the operation's kingpin, J. Irwin Miller. Basically, there's a move afoot to have Cummins Engine make additional shares of stock available to the public, slightly reducing the Miller family's stake in the company. I have to work up a case for why that's necessary, as well as outline how much stock should be offered, and my analysis will be presented to Miller.

"Getting Mr. Miller to agree to this is going to be akin to absconding with his firstborn child," Higgins warns me as I polish my report for Miller. "It's going to take a lot of cajoling and selling."

I'm invariably upbeat, but a little negative thought sprints through my brain before I can corral it: Am I being roped into a politically sensitive, potential suicide mission that would only be given to the new guy in case the whole thing goes terribly awry?

That little burp of negativism disappears as quickly as it materializes, and I get back to the task at hand. After I submit my report to

Higgins, he gives it back to me with directions to make a few minor revisions. I'm off to a good start.

My second assignment puts me in direct contact with Miller for the first time. Our encounter takes place thanks to the fact that I'm working with First Boston, the investment banking firm doing the road show for the Cummins stock offering. Thanks to my role, a one-on-one meeting between Miller and me is scheduled.

Even though I've never interacted with Miller, I have a pretty good idea what his shtick is all about—undoubtedly a textbook Type A personality who's probably hard-charging, no-nonsense, and sharp-tongued to boot. I'm pleasantly surprised when I meet J. Irwin Miller, a very tall man with a long face, pointed chin, and thinning gray hair. Mild-mannered and soft-spoken, he couldn't have a sweeter, more unassuming personality!

Along with not prejudging people, I learn another valuable lesson: You don't have to carry on like a demonic despot to lead a successful business enterprise. Intimidating the heck out of employees and brow beating them isn't necessary to reap maximum performance.

To this day, my management style at Brown Capital Management still displays traces of what I learned during my days in Columbus with the self-effacing, understated, and always engaged J. Irwin Miller.

★   ★   ★

Something happens during my second week at Irwin Management Co. that has stuck with me my entire life.

I'm in my second-floor office on the Saturday that ends my second week, dutifully dealing with matters related to the First Boston stock offering. I happen to casually glance up from my desk and I notice a bunch of folks calmly sauntering down Washington Street donned in white sheets and hoods. Just outside the walls of my office, a massive Ku Klux Klan gathering has materialized in the streets of Columbus!

When Harold Higgins was extolling Columbus' architecture, its many beautiful parks, Midwestern values, and low cost of living, he somehow forgot to mention that it's apparently a KKK hotbed. When I was growing up in Apopka, Florida, the black community talked about the Klan, but I never actually saw them. Seeing these cretins up close and personal for the first time is a tremendously unsettling experience.

Obviously I'm concerned for my safety, but I'm more worried about Sylvia and the girls. I hope I haven't gotten us all into something none of us bargained for by moving to Columbus.

Hunching down at my desk, so that Irwin Management's newest African-American worker isn't spotted by the hooded cowards rallying just outside my window, I hurriedly dial my wife on my desk phone.

"Sylvia," I whisper, even though I'm in no danger of being overheard. "The Ku Klux Klan is outside Irwin Management. They're outside my building!"

"What!"

"The Klan. The KKK. They're holding a rally on Washington Street. There's about a hundred of them."

"Eddie, are you okay? They're not in the building, are they?"

"No, I'm safe. There's nothing going on near the house, is it?"

As I talk to Sylvia, I can hear a chant of some kind rising from the street. Fortunately, the voices sound calm and unexcited. Still, their effect on me is absolutely chilling. And it's enraging to think that simply because I wanted to get some work done on my First Boston assignment, my well-being has to be imperiled thanks to the proceedings outside. While I'm inside Irwin Management trying to help my family take full advantage of the American Dream and trying to help society by eventually donating to charity, the robed wonders outside are pandering to peoples' basest fears.

"Eddie," Sylvia says, sounding utterly terrified, "please don't go outside!"

Given that I didn't wake up harboring a death wish, and haven't acquired one since arriving at work, I really don't think my dear wife needs to worry about that.

"Sweetie, I'll call you when these clowns are gone," I say, trying my best to sound blithe and unconcerned. Obviously, I'm terrifically concerned. And I'm quietly seething, angry at the people outside making a mockery of the First Amendment, and angry that no one at Irwin Management alerted me to this kind of thing.

Eventually the Klan disappears back beneath the cow patties and rocks they sprang from under, and I'm able to warily walk out the front door and depart Irwin Management.

After getting back home, Sylvia and I have a talk about Columbus, Indiana, and its KKK members. I assure her that if she's the least bit concerned about her or our daughters' safety, I'll have moving vans roll up on Monday morning. And I mean that.

But my soul mate is not the least bit rattled or intimidated. She feels that Columbus hasn't cornered the market on crackpots and racial bigots, and that a certain segment of the population in Connecticut, or California, or even Alaska, is going to behave the same way.

I'm totally in accord with that. Racists ran my grandfather out of Ocoee, Florida, and stole two hundred acres of his land, reducing him to a menial laborer for the rest of his life. I'll be damned if Columbus, Indiana's, small-minded contingent is going to run me out of town.

When I return to Irwin Management on Monday, it's as if Saturday's KKK march was a bad dream, a mere figment of my imagination. No one utters a word about the hundred or so robed Klansmen who brazenly paraded past my office window over the weekend, so I play the game myself and act as if nothing happened.

But before the close of business, just to ensure that I haven't gone stark raving mad, I go to the office of Irwin Management's only other African-American, as well as the man responsible for getting me into the firm, Clarence Malone. I gently shut Clarence's door behind me, and all pretense immediately flies out the window. He knows exactly why I'm paying him a visit, and is clearly chagrined.

"Eddie, I heard what happened, man," Clarence says, motioning for me to take a seat. "Sylvia called my wife. I swear to you that in the year or so I've been here, I've never seen anything like that. The Ku Klux Klan marching down the middle of the damned street! I'm so sorry."

"Clarence, why are you apologizing?" I ask my distraught friend and colleague. "There are mean, ignorant people in every state in the union. I just had to make sure I wasn't hallucinating or something."

"There are some really good human beings here, Eddie," Clarence replies. "I know that for a fact. And they know J. Irwin Miller is serious as a heart attack about integrating this place, and Cummins

Engine, too. I'm sure people here are mortified and embarrassed about that Klan march, and don't know what to say. So they don't say anything.

"No one has mentioned it to me, either!" Clarence adds.

That conversation marks the last time I mention the Klan march to anyone, including Sylvia. My makeup just doesn't allow me to dwell on negatives. However, every time I go to a bank or grocery store or gas station right after the KKK assembly, I always look at the courteous individual waiting on me and wonder: *Were you there?*

One of the best things about the assistant to the office of the president position is that it gives me a view of Irwin Management from 50,000 feet. I'm continually interfacing with the various groups within the firm, giving me a good feel for how the entire entity functions.

During his sales pitch to me, Harold Higgins repeatedly emphasized that not only would I have an opportunity to observe the entire operation, but I'd be able to interact with all the pieces. He said that would give me an excellent sense of which group I'd like to eventually move into, and he was right.

The other thing Higgins said several times when he was recruiting me was that having good people skills was absolutely critical, because not only would I have to get along with the various groups, but I would need to coexist smoothly with the Miller family from time to time. That turned out to be on the money also.

It hasn't taken me long to see that the asset allocation folks tend to be very cerebral, measured, and methodical. They sit around all day running various financial models that take into account tax considerations, what portion of the Miller family's assets should be invested into various investment vehicles, that sort of thing. I'm not the impulsive type, but I also don't like to study things to death before taking action, so I don't think asset allocation would be my cup of tea when I'm no longer assistant to the office of the president. So that gets scratched off my list.

Far more action-oriented are the guys in the real estate group. They're a hard-charging, deal-cutting bunch with a cowboy mentality. I think they have more fun than anyone else in Irwin Management, and are the freest spirits. They certainly tell the bawdiest jokes.

Real estate interests me as a personal investment vehicle, as evidenced by the fact that Sylvia and I purchased rental properties in Poughkeepsie. But it doesn't interest me enough to make the real estate group a potential landing spot.

As for Irwin Management's oil and gas mavens, the only time I come in contact with them is by phone, and I have no desire to move to Houston.

The consulting group, which prepares mission papers for J. Irwin Miller, is very, very slow-paced, measured, and methodical. It doesn't take long to ascertain that consulting doesn't particularly pique my interest.

I like the marketable securities group. Like real estate, the guys in marketable securities are action-oriented and hard-charging. They have to be, because the vagaries of the stock market mean they work in one of the most fluid and dynamic environments imaginable. Real estate developments generally move with glacial speed, but with the stock market you can lose a fortune in a matter of minutes.

Another reason I'm attracted to marketable securities is because I love investing and have done quite well with the little portfolio I put together on my own. So I follow a two-pronged plan that hopefully will eventually land me in marketable securities.

First and foremost, I do the best possible job I can as assistant to the office of the president. But I also make it a point to strike up a relationship with Garnett Keith, who heads marketable securities. I make it crystal clear to him, and to Harold Higgins, that in a perfect world I'd love to move to marketable securities.

How does the old adage go—ask and you shall receive? After a year and a half as assistant to the office of the president—during which I receive exemplary evaluations—I'm transferred to marketable securities. To be more accurate, a position is created for me that allows me to wear several caps. Perfect!

It takes the efforts of roughly seven people to ensure that marketable securities is a smooth-running, efficient operation. At least three toil in the trenches researching companies whose stock Irwin Management has an interest in. There's also a trader, someone who takes care of client relations, Garnett Keith, and me. In my new position, which I'm absolutely ecstatic about, the operations side of the group and trading report to me.

But here's the icing on the cake—they want me to manage marketable securities' cash, which is a sum in the millions. I'm responsible for finding the best short-term instruments to put liquid assets into. However, before I finish my first week in my new post, I'm already trying to figure out how I can have responsibility for a portion of the common stock portfolio. In other words, I want to have "yea or nay" authority when it comes to deciding what stocks Irwin Management should invest in.

I have a knack for investing, am making money with my personal portfolio, and I want to ply my skills on a much larger stage. A stage where someone else's money will be able to benefit from the impressive returns I'm enjoying privately.

But in the investment business, obviously you don't just walk in off the street and start making multi-million dollar investments with other peoples' money. First, you're placed under an electron microscope so that your methodologies and personality can be vigorously scrutinized and dissected. That's what I'm going through now.

Everybody in marketable securities is getting a feel for this Eddie Brown guy who only joined the firm a year and a half ago. That's not much time at all when millions of Miller family dollars could potentially be adversely impacted.

I don't mind the close inspection—in fact, I welcome it. Because I'm reasonably confident that as people peel back my layers and evaluate my makeup and core competence, they'll like what they see. In the meantime, I'm learning something new about investing and securities with each passing day.

The various responsibilities I have within the marketable securities group are allowing me to become quite familiar with how it works. I'm getting a soup-to-nuts familiarization with Irwin Management's investment arm.

Every day I walk out the front door of Irwin Management to return home to Sylvia and my girls, I feel a few steps closer to having the tools that will allow me to secure my family's financial security and replicate Lady B.'s charitable largesse. And I can't wait to return to work every morning.

When I was assistant to the office of the president, I felt that I had a very good job. However, making the switch to marketable securities has made me one of those rare individuals who is fortunate enough to work in a profession they truly enjoy.

Since I have a fair amount of autonomy regarding how I divvy up my workday, I make it a point to spend a fair amount of time with the securities trader on my team. I've never done trading before, and I want to understand precisely what traders do, to the point where I feel I could actually do the job myself if necessary.

So for a couple of months I totally immerse myself in the ins and outs of trading. Here's a thumbnail: After a portfolio manager makes decisions on what they want to buy or sell for their portfolio, the trader is responsible for getting those orders executed in an orderly fashion, and at the best price.

Along with those considerations, traders must execute orders in a manner that doesn't disrupt the stock market. For example, if you have a significant position in a thinly-traded stock, it's necessary to feed your order in increments, lest your actions adversely affect the market.

At Irwin Management, a typical position would be tens of thousands, or hundreds of thousands, of shares. Want to know the beauty of all this securities stuff? For me, it's fun. It doesn't even seem as though I'm working. It feels as though I'm engaged in my all-time favorite hobby and getting paid to do it.

Each passing day reinforces that I have found the one thing that I want to spend the rest of my working days pursuing. Electrical engineering was interesting and mildly gratifying, but never scintillating and captivating like dealing with marketable securities.

I'm being taught how to eventually generate an awful lot of money for myself *and* I'm being paid to learn. It's such a deliciously wonderful situation that sometimes I laugh out loud in my car while driving home. Not only do I feel incredibly blessed, but I feel a heightened obligation to give back to society once wealth is within my grasp.

Life is going well for me outside of Irwin Management, too. Later in life, people often ask if I felt I was paying my dues by living in Columbus, Indiana, and I can honestly say that wasn't the case. It wasn't a hardship posting by any stretch of the imagination. Excluding the KKK event that transpired right after I moved into town, it's proven to be a great place to raise a family. I might not feel this way if I were single, or if Sylvia and I didn't have any children.

On those occasions when my wife and I want a taste of city life, as well as a parents night out, Indianapolis is about 40 miles to the north, while Cincinnati is roughly 75 miles to the south. These excursions are rare and most of our time is spent in Columbus.

We've made a lot of friends here and are regulars in a bowling league that descends on a local bowling alley every Sunday evening. In keeping with our personalities, my dear wife is more concerned with having fun and relaxing when the 10 pins start flying. Whereas I'm looking to quietly, decisively steamroll my opponents when scores are tallied.

You'd better believe J. Irwin Miller is keeping score when Irwin Management quarterly reports are issued. IBM is certainly keeping score when computer sales are analyzed across its various product lines. I'm in the same mode—out to ensure that things add up in my favor when all is said and done.

I guess that's what has drawn me toward golf, along with the fact that most of the men at Irwin Management play. But the other thing about me is that I won't get in any game unless I can acquit myself with competitive, masterful performances. My M.O. is to learn the fundamentals and master them, then come out and slaughter opponents in a very quiet, low-key way. It's not necessary to talk smack, because when you're killing somebody in a head-to-head contest, that pretty much says it all.

This doesn't mean I'm not enjoying my dominance—I'm relishing every single second. But until I get to the point where my game is capable of speaking for me on the golf course, I refuse to take on challengers. Instead, I've bought myself some clubs and take lessons at a beautiful Columbus golf course called Otter Creek.

There's another reason I'm not disappearing for three and four hours at a pop to golf with my colleagues from Irwin Management, and that's because my wife has put her foot down and said "heck no!" In case I haven't fully gotten the message, Sylvia warns me in no uncertain terms that she doesn't wish to be a golf widow.

So I limit my golf activities to practice sessions and keep the peace, patiently awaiting the day when Tonya and Jennifer are big enough for me to enjoy carefree afternoons on the links. All things in time. If I can be a delayed-gratification kind of guy when it comes to building wealth, I think golf can wait, too.

You may recall that I tried to fly helicopters in the Army, but couldn't due to my vision. Well the aviation bug must have clamped down on me pretty good, because I've started taking pilot lessons at an airport not far from our house. I hold my breath when I inform Sylvia of this.

I get a kiss on the forehead, and an admonition that my desire to learn to fly was "as crazy as two left shoes" when I have "two little brats" at home. I wait for that to be followed by a blanket moratorium on aviation, but it never comes. So I'm still learning how to fly a single-engine Cessna 172, which is a very enjoyable and challenging endeavor.

I don't know, maybe being an aviation widow is preferable to being a golf widow? I don't profess to fully understand how my wife's mind operates, and I suspect she feels the same way about mine. But what we agree on is that we have a great marriage, we view each other as best friends, and we're pretty pleased with how we're rearing our beautiful little girls. And we love each other deeply.

Life is good, very good. So what better time to toss out another life-altering curveball?

Chapter 12

Pulling the Trigger on Investments

J. Irwin Miller monitors the clicking of an internal clock.

And everyone at Irwin Management is keenly aware that when his timepiece gets to a certain point, there will probably be a profound impact on our livelihoods.

For some reason, Miller has decreed that once employees of Irwin Management, Cummins Engine, and Irwin Union Bank & Trust reach 65, they need to be put out to pasture. Mothballed. Retired.

Personally, I fail to see the wisdom in this, because I know people 65 and older who are still vital and active and who have an awful lot of wisdom and experience to impart. After I start my own firm I continue to work into my seventies and have treasured investment professionals on my team who are older than I am.

However, Miller's the kingpin around Irwin Management Co., and does as he pleases.

It's currently May 1973 and Miller happens to be 63. I figure that when he turns 65 and steps down from the chairmanship of Irwin Management and Cummins Engine, he's not going to need

85 Irwin Management employees to oversee his family's assets and provide financial services. He'll have enough free time to take care of some of those functions himself, if he so pleases.

I've been at Irwin Management going on three years now, and I consider myself pretty fluent in regard to the language and operations of marketable securities. That's not to say that I don't have more to learn—there's always more to learn. But I feel as though I'm ready to become a portfolio manager, giving me green-light authority in terms of allocating millions of dollars to make investments.

I don't have that authority at Irwin Management, so I'm starting to think that it may be an opportune time to bring my tenure with the firm to a close. Stock trading and research are second nature for me now, and my stock-picking skills have progressed to the point where I can sniff out a dog—or a winner—a mile away.

The firm has basically been my financial finishing school after receiving my MBA from Indiana University. I've grown professionally and personally at Irwin Management, and Columbus has turned out to be a pretty neat place to live. However, my career ambitions, combined with the fact that J. Irwin Miller is retiring in two years, have convinced me that it's time to start looking for the next job opportunity.

So I've been quietly looking around for firms that that will give me the power to pull the trigger on stock investment ideas. That's the next logical step in my career progression. I'm also looking at firms that have a much larger client base than a single family.

I've even got my search criterion in pretty sharp focus: Which firm is the best among large firms concentrating on the growth style of investing?

After researching and investigating a number of financial firms, I find Baltimore-based T. Rowe Price the most interesting. Why? Because they basically created the growth stock theory of investing that I find so fascinating. Why not go to the firm that originated it?

When Thomas Rowe Price Jr. started T. Rowe Price in Baltimore in 1937, he felt that an asset management firm, as separate and distinct from a securities brokerage firm, would better serve the needs of his clients. He also felt that charging clients a fixed fee based on assets under management, as opposed to a commission based on transactions, would be an ideal way to dovetail the interests of clients and managers. Under this arrangement, as a client's assets grow in value, the manager's revenues increase accordingly.

Charging a fee based on assets under management is something I will incorporate in my own firm—Brown Capital Management—decades later. I also concentrate on stocks with impressive growth potential, a style of investment management pioneered by Mr. Price.

In a nutshell, 1970s investors drawn to growth stocks are looking for companies they think can grow their sales and earnings per share faster than the overall stock market, or the Standard & Poor's 500. Investment managers who concentrate on growth stocks put most of their focus on the income statement.

By way of contrast, managers of what are known as value stocks are forever on the prowl for companies with hidden value, or assets, that aren't being properly valued by the marketplace.

For me growth is the way to go, but I don't happen to know anyone at T. Rowe Price, nor have I ever spent any time in Baltimore. So my solution is to write a letter to the president of T. Rowe Price, Charles Schaefer.

Making it a point to keep my missive one page long, I inform Schaefer that I have a strong hunch that Irwin Management will be dramatically downsized after J. Irwin Miller reaches 65, so I'm currently casting about for other employment possibilities. Furthermore, I find T. Rowe Price's growth style of investing immensely attractive, and am interested in working for the firm as a portfolio manager.

Within the confines of my one-pager, I also note that I have an MBA from Indiana University, a master's in electrical engineering from New York University, and have also worked for IBM as an engineer. At no point in the letter do I make reference to anything that might indicate that I'm black. I would prefer that Schaefer and his people contact me based on what I feel is a very strong CV. I feel that I have experience and training that should make me stand out among other T. Rowe Price's applicants, irrespective of race.

Please don't think that I'm naïve or deluded here—I've been a clear beneficiary of affirmative action up to this point, and I'm not ashamed or reticent in the least when it comes to acknowledging that fact. But having had the door cracked open for me, starting with Lady

B. subsidizing my undergraduate tuition, I feel that I've been able to establish an outstanding track record that stands on its on merits. And it's on that basis that I want T. Rowe Price to evaluate my candidacy.

Several weeks unfold before I hear back from the investment firm I consider the originator of growth stocks. When they do reply, it's with a warm letter from the individual heading their investment counseling division, which is comprised of portfolio managers who oversee the assets of T. Rowe Price's private clients and also manage the firm's mutual funds.

The return letter indicates that T. Rowe Price has some degree of interest in my unsolicited query, so would I please be kind enough to send them more detailed information about my experiences at Irwin Management?

You better believe it!

Able to type 60 words a minute thanks to the typing lessons Grandma had me take back in Apopka, Florida, I tap out another letter to T. Rowe Price. Instead of a pithy one-page deal, this time I forward a five-page treatise on how I have helped research companies for Irwin Management's marketable securities group, and have even pinch hit as a trader.

But the bulk of my letter underscores my successes at identifying stocks that have enjoyed impressive growth for J. Irwin Miller and his company. Leaving no stone unturned, I even lay out my stock-picking methodologies and prerequisites for the folks at T. Rowe Price.

A smile is on my face as I drop the second letter into a mailbox. I'm reasonably certain T. Rowe Price doesn't often receive thoughtful five-page letters from prospective portfolio managers who just happen to be huge fans of the firm's growth stock philosophy. I'm hoping my correspondence will result in an interview.

So it's a good idea to tee this up for The Boss' benefit before I hear back from T. Rowe Price. I won't be terribly shocked if Sylvia informs me that she's not crazy about the prospect of uprooting the family from Columbus.

One evening after we've had dinner and the girls have been put to bed, I grab my wife by the hand and lead her outside, to make darn sure sensitive Tonya doesn't hear our conversation.

And then I talk to Sylvia about my need to grow professionally, and how if I'm able to pull the trigger on investment ideas, that will put me in a different league regarding my ability to secure our family's financial future. A bit of a stretch, yes, but it sounds perfectly plausible and reasonable coming out of my mouth. To me, anyway.

Realizing that something's up, Sylvia is giving me a look that's best described as somewhat suspicious, with a dollop of skepticism thrown in for good measure.

"You're thinking about moving again, aren't you Eddie?' she asks quietly as we sit on the front porch. Bringing my sparkling sales pitch to a screeching halt.

"Not just for the sake of moving, honey," I reply. "Give me a little credit—there's usually a method to my madness!"

Sylvia just keeps staring at the starry Indiana sky, and I join her. In light of the silence that greeted my little stab at humor, it's time to push the mute button. Happily married couples know when it's time to keep forging ahead conversationally, and when it's time to shut the heck up.

"Where are you looking?" my spouse asks. "It seems like we just moved here from Indiana University!"

"I'm looking at a firm in Baltimore called T. Rowe Price. They're to the investing world what Yale or Harvard is to education. I wrote them and they seemed kind of interested, so they asked me to write a little bit more about my background and what they think I might bring to their firm."

"Which is?"

Hearing a rustling noise behind us, we both turn simultaneously to see a little brown elf standing with her hands pressed against the screen door. Sylvia and I immediately scuttle our conversation and Sylvia rises to put Tonya back in bed.

"Why are you two outside in the dark? Isn't it impossible to see?" Tonya asks with such unassailable logic that it feels like a question from a 30-year-old woman camping out in the body of a seven-year-old.

It just so happens that dad can see things just fine, little one. I was trying to help your mom see the light before you interrupted my roll!

Waiting for Sylvia to return as I gaze up at the stars, I feel the same little twinges of guilt that I felt before moving my family from

Poughkeepsie to Indiana. That's because I know that if we pull up roots in Columbus, Indiana, and move to Baltimore or wherever, it's going to be a disruptive experience.

Sure, it'll be all about short-term pain to achieve long-term gain, but whose gain? Yeah, we'll all benefit, but again I have to ask myself exactly what I hope to achieve with T. Rowe Price? I gaze up at the Milky Way and, despite myself, think back to Tonya's stuttering episode after we left Poughkeepsie.

Sylvia comes back outside and sits beside me on the porch.

"Why did she wake up?" I ask, genuinely curious why our oldest daughter arose in the middle of our conversation.

"I don't know, Eddie. But that girl's got some sensitive antenna."

Not sure if that last comment is an innocent statement of fact, a low blow, or a little of both, I change the subject.

"Honey, I've been saying that they're probably going to take a broom to Irwin Management after Mr. Miller turns 65. I really believe that, so rather than sit here and wait for the ax to fall, it makes sense to me to start talking to folks now."

"It's not just that. You want to be in a position to call the shots when it comes to investment decisions."

"True."

Sighing softly, Sylvia crosses her arms and looks down momentarily at the wooden porch. Oh no, not this again. I thought we were past this!

"I really like the school Tonya is in," Sylvia starts off. "And it took a long time to get Jennifer in that church day care."

Not quite sure what might constitute a safe response, I opt for the safe default position and say nothing.

"I kind of like small-town life," Sylvia continues. "I grew up in a small town and . . . Baltimore? Who wants to move to Baltimore? It's a place you drive through while you're going somewhere else. I don't think I want to live in a big city."

"We drive to Indianapolis and Cincinnati all the time," I counter, only to be reminded that we don't live in either of those places. As the conversation unfolds, I manage to assuage Sylvia's fears about Baltimore, which is pretty good considering that I've never set foot in the city myself.

And I promise her that wherever I move next, we will stay there for at least five to ten years. Because I think part of what's bothering Sylvia is that our existence is starting to have a distinctly nomadic quality to it, and that doesn't set well with her nesting instinct.

One area where Sylvia and I see eye-to-eye is with my frustration at not having green-light power when it comes to making common stock investments. She wants me to have that because, like me, she feels I deserve it. Sylvia also doesn't like the uncertainty associated with J. Irwin Miller's impending retirement, and what that may mean for Irwin Management Co. and for our family.

Before we turn in for the night, Sylvia and I reach an understanding that if things become serious with T. Rowe Price, she'll back me on the move to Baltimore. My wonderful wife has finally come to the realization that she married an ambitious, intellectually curious man who's a bit of a rolling stone.

A few more weeks go by before I hear from T. Rowe Price. A second letter from the firm explains that one of their investment teams is considering adding a portfolio manager, and gives me a date and time for conducting an interview in Baltimore.

T. Rowe Price flies me to Baltimore and puts me up in a hotel that's within walking distance from its downtown corporate offices. I have what I consider to be a very informative interview with an investment team that only has two members, instead of the four or five that most T. Rowe Price investment teams typically have. Seems the timing of my inquiry to the firm is excellent.

In its 1973 iteration, T. Rowe Price has $6 billion under management, and $4 billion of that is from the assets of private clients, pension funds, and endowment funds. The remaining $2 billion is tied up in mutual funds, investment vehicles T. Rowe Price only has four of.

Fast forward to 2011 and you'll find that the bulk of T. Rowe Price's assets under management come from its involvement with mutual funds.

When I travel to T. Rowe Price, I notice striking similarities with Irwin Management. Once again, most of the investment professionals have MBAs from Harvard, Stanford, and the Wharton School. Few in the tiers of upper management at T. Rowe Price seemed to be from Baltimore, just as almost no one at Irwin Management is from Columbus, Indiana.

As I sit in the waiting area at T. Rowe Price prior to being interviewed, I can't help but reflect how the cookie-cutter hiring practices at the nation's top investment firms make it incredibly difficult—if not impossible—for African Americans to enter the business. That epiphany is accompanied not by rancor but by sadness, because the industry is clinging to patterns that routinely deny it of extraordinary talent.

Eventually I'm fetched by Bill Shepherd, one of the two portfolio managers on the team with the opening. A smoker with a medium build and a full head of hair, Bill is curious to know why I want to get into investment management, which I find a bit of an odd question. We also talk generally about my experiences in life, and what Bill will be looking for in whoever his team hires.

Maybe I'm waaaay off base, but I have a sense that a courtship is underway!

My next meeting is with Bill's colleague, Dan Dent, who's easily 6-foot-4, full-bodied, and balding. Dan comes across as very thoughtful, even a tad professorial, and like Bill he asks questions whose purpose seem to be to help him get a handle on whether he would feel comfortable working with me.

Dan's first two or three queries probe my investment business acumen, and once it's clear that I'm up to speed in that regard, Dan quickly segues to topics of a more general nature. One area where I feel like I'm falling down with Dan and Bill is professional sports. I'm conversant, but don't really follow my inquisitors' beloved Baltimore Colts or Orioles, because there's no reason for me to in Columbus, Indiana!

Even so, I'm feeling pretty positive about how things went as I leave T. Rowe Price's offices on my way to Baltimore's airport. It's clear to me that instead of being flown in for some perfunctory interview, I was subjected to a preliminary sniff test to see if I might be a suitable candidate to become the firm's first African-American investment professional.

People often ask do I find being a racial trailblazer a daunting proposition? No, not really! Once the novelty of my skin's melanin content wears off, performance and competence are what carry the day. Based on what I've seen of T. Rowe Price thus far, I think I cannot only hold my own, but could prove to be an asset.

Anyway, when it comes to one and only status, I'm surprised—and disappointed—that's still an issue in 1973. And I pray that Tonya and Jennifer don't confront these same issues when they're my age.

About two weeks pass by before I hear anything from T. Rowe Price. When they do contact me, it's with an offer to return to Baltimore for a second round of interviews.

During the second go round, I meet with the leaders of other investment teams, culminating with a dinner in a downtown Baltimore restaurant with Dan Dent and Bill Shepherd. The dinner conversation settles on a subject I could talk about for hours on end—my approach to investing and what thought processes I go through in the course of determining which companies are suitable to invest in. I'm at my most effusive and animated when talking about investing, and I'm sure that Dan and Bill can plainly see my passion.

While they're getting a read on me, I'm also checking them out to see if they're people I would want to work long hours with in an office setting. Fairly guarded and close to the vest during my first trip to Baltimore, the two of them are a lot more open, collegial, and relaxed the second time around.

The vibe at dinner is excellent, and it's abundantly clear to me that I could comfortably work with these two men. I'm growing kind of excited about the prospect of working for T. Rowe Price as a portfolio manager, and hope I'm offered the position on Dan and Bill's team.

A few more weeks go by before T. Rowe Price contacts me about flying to Baltimore for a third time, this time with Sylvia in tow. It's investment industry practice to be very, very deliberate when it comes to giving prospective employees a once over. So spouses are invariably included in the process, partially to see if they'll fit in with a firm's corporate culture, and partially to make sure they've signed off on their husband or wife taking the position in question.

You don't want someone you've just hired to make multi-million dollar decisions to be distracted at work because their disgruntled spouse didn't want them to take the job in the first place. For both parties' sakes, it's critical to get investment-industry hiring decisions right. Investment teams spend an awful lot of time in each others' company and absolutely have to work smoothly together, so you don't want to rush into what will be a very high-stakes marriage.

Still, the fact that T. Rowe Price is flying Sylvia with me this time is a very, very good sign. I figure that as long as I don't do anything crazy during my time in Baltimore, like speak in tongues or blow my nose onto my shirt sleeve, the transition to becoming a portfolio manager is pretty well in the bag.

When Sylvia and I get to Baltimore, she's hustled off by several T. Rowe Price wives for a tour of the city's neighborhoods, as well as the other things that make Baltimore a welcoming place to live. Fantastic! The fact that they've been recruited to convince my wife that Baltimore is a good locale to put down roots is a very encouraging sign.

Meanwhile, my time during the third visit to T. Rowe Price is overwhelmingly spent with Dan Dent and Bill Shepherd, who give me an opportunity to ask any questions or voice any concerns that I may have. Very pro forma stuff, but naturally I maintain my game face, keep my guard up, and remain on my toes. I've heard of too many third interviews where a seemingly innocuous comment by the person being interviewed led to their candidacy being scuttled. That's not happening to me.

The day is capped off by a nice dinner attended by Dan, Bill, me, and our wives. Afterward, when Sylvia and I are back in our hotel room, we both agree that it looks as though my next stop is going to be T. Rowe Price. Sylvia, who had a marvelous time with the T. Rowe Price wives, gives me her unqualified blessing, which is a huge relief. Because without that, I'm not going anywhere.

Having gotten a feel for T. Rowe Price's *modus operandi*, I predict that in about two or three weeks I'll be receiving a letter with their decision. When it finally arrives, I waste little time opening it as soon as I get home from Irwin Management. The letter is the one I had hoped for, offering me a portfolio manager's job on Dan and Bill's team, at a very generous salary and with a tremendously impressive benefits package.

I'm pleased about both of those things, but what excites me most is that I will finally be calling the shots regarding investment decisions.

To me, that's the most attractive inducement of all to leave Irwin Management Co. for T. Rowe Price.

Three years after earning my MBA, I'm finally on a playing field where the biggest boys in the investment business hang out. If I perform well at T. Rowe Price, which is widely viewed as one of the world's top investment firms, my reputation will be golden.

It's not overstating things that I have just landed the opportunity of a lifetime, and I enjoy a giddy sense of euphoria that easily lasts a good week after I accept T. Rowe Price's offer. This is what I had envisioned when I quit my job at IBM and dragged my family halfway across the United States five years ago.

I give praise to God for vindicating me and for ordering my steps in a way that have made my move to T. Rowe Price possible.

Thanks to my handsome remuneration and the impressive investment perks the firm makes available to its employees, at the age of 32 I've arrived at a place where the tools and the capital to solidify my family's financial security will both be within my grasp. I'm also a significant step closer to fulfilling my pledge to Lady B.

In keeping with my new station in life, when I make the move to Baltimore the operation won't be one of my infamous U-Haul specials. My new employers pay to have a moving van pack up my house and haul my family's belongings back East, making this deal a lot less traumatic for Sylvia, Tonya, and Jennifer.

However, regardless of how diligently we may try to position things, ultimately life has a way of lining our roads with unanticipated bumps and potholes. In the midst of preparing to move to Baltimore, Sylvia is knocked for a loop when her wonderful mother, Carmen Thurston, passes away unexpectedly of natural causes in her hometown of King William, Virginia.

Mrs. Thurston was my wife's touchstone on every topic from A to Z and Sylvia does not take her mother's passing well. Nor do I, for that matter. T. Rowe Price is instantly relegated from being my end all and be all to a backburner issue. The financial industry is an important part of my life but it's not the most important thing in my life, a distinction made clear to me during the tumult my family experienced after I left IBM.

After Sylvia, Tonya, Jennifer, and I make a heart-aching journey to Virginia for Mrs. Thurston's funeral and return to Columbus, our impending move serves as a tremendously welcome distraction for Sylvia. Despite her remaining misgivings about Baltimore, she throws herself heart and soul into making sure our move comes off smoothly.

It takes virtually no time to sell our very nice three-bedroom contemporary house in Columbus. In fact, we receive an offer before we actually move. Our home sells for around $41,000, putting a nice profit in our pockets and further stoking my appreciation of real estate's wealth-building potential.

Sylvia and I look at Baltimore homes costing up to three times what our 3,500-square-foot Columbus house did, but we can't find anything comparable in terms of square footage or quality. So we basically downsize in Baltimore, buying a smaller home than the one we enjoyed in Indiana. The plan is to save our money, with an eye toward eventually buying a suburban lot that we'll build on a few years from now.

Slightly leery of our new city's public school system, Sylvia's fears are validated when she finds out that the elementary school in our new neighborhood packs 40 students in each classroom.

That generates a bit of tension and consternation in my household, but Sylvia and I know better than to discuss the matter in front of the girls. We're never going down that road again if we can help it. The situation is remedied by enrolling Tonya in private school, and we follow that up by registering her in a gymnastics class at a nearby YMCA as well.

We put Jennifer into a different private school afterward, calling for Sylvia to perform yeoman chauffeur duty, and we also find a church home with a Presbyterian congregation that appeals to Sylvia and I and that has an excellent Sunday school. Now that we're somewhat plugged into Baltimore's landscape, and Sylvia appears to be happy with our transformation, I can start work at T. Rowe Price and give it the focus and dedication it deserves.

I had put off my first day by a couple of months in order to ensure that my three lovely ladies were ideally situated before I walk through T. Rowe Price's front door for the first time.

By the way, I turned out to be correct regarding J. Irwin Miller's retirement and the effect that would have on Irwin Management Co.

My habit of declining to smile for photographs was in full force as a very dapper three-year-old in Apopka, Florida.

My teacher, Mildred Board, made me king of my third-grade class while Elizabeth Wagner, to my left, was queen. I'm still awaiting the coronation ceremony.

Direct from Allentown High School, the Cooltones singing group, comprised of (from left), Jay Proctor, Arnold Drayton, "Butch" Ransom, me, and "Baby" Enix.

At Fort Monmouth, New Jersey, doing my part to ensure that democratic ideals aren't imperiled by the marauding Red Threat of the early 1960s.

A date that will live in infamy, August 11, 1962, with the former Sylvia Thurston in King William, Virginia.

Sylvia and I celebrating our first wedding anniversary at the Moulin Rouge cabaret in Paris, along with friend Fred Hall.

This shot, taken with T. Rowe Price colleagues during a conference in Hot Springs, Virginia, speaks volumes about financial-industry diversity back in 1973.

The 30th anniversary of *Wall $treet Week with Louis Rukeyser* provided me with an opportunity to ring the opening New York Stock Exchange bell in 2000.

Here I am conferring with Harold Higgins, the wonderful executive who recruited me into Irwin Management Company, in Columbus, Indiana.

I'm elated following my first *Wall $treet Week with Louis Rukeyser* appearance with (from left), Bob Stovall, Louis Rukeyser, Julius Westheimer, and Carter Randall in 1978.

In the inscription, Louis Rukeyser pays homage to Brown Capital Management's growth at a reasonable price (GARP) investment philosophy.

Helping Jennifer commemorate her Ph.D. from the University of Miami are (from left), Sylvia; grandson Elias; Jennifer; my mother, Annie Mae Brown; and Tonya.

Joining me in Apopka, Florida, during the dedication of a memorial garden for my mother in 2004 are my son-in-law, Kempton; Tonya; grandsons Darrell, Jr. and Elias; Jennifer; Sylvia; and son-in-law, Darrell.

Pursuing our love of the outdoors are Tonya, Sylvia, Jennifer and I during a cycling trip in Italy in 1991.

My inimitable uncle, Jake Brown, Jr., in a picture taken in Apopka, Florida, around 2000.

The joy of finally being able to conduct business inside Brown Capital Management's first Baltimore office was sufficient to coax a rare smiling photo out of me.
Photo Credit: John McGrail

Sylvia and I posing with local, state, and national leaders during a ribbon cutting for the Enoch Pratt Free Library's Eddie and Sylvia Brown African American Collection, in Baltimore in 2003.
Photo Credit: Jay L. Baker

Sylvia and I taking advantage of an opportunity to pose with one of my personal heroes, South African Archbishop Desmond Tutu, who was visiting Baltimore in 2008.

My wife and I manage to get in the same frame with another of my personal heroes, Berkshire Hathaway Chairman Warren Buffett, during a trip to Las Vegas.

staffing levels. He didn't give a certain date for people to terminate their employment after he turned 65, but did make it clear that a number of positions were being eliminated. Miller gave those who were let go as much time as they needed to find new jobs, and it took some a year to nail down suitable employment. Sad news, because Irwin Management really had a family feel and I made some enduring friendships there.

It remains to be seen if T. Rowe Price is capable of approximating Irwin Management's wonderful corporate culture. I start working at Price in July 1973 and have a distinct sense that many of my colleagues are very curious about the new kid on the block. Partially because no other new equity manager has ever looked like me, but also because I think I'm one of the first to saunter in without the usual Harvard or Stanford or Wharton pedigree.

I'll give Bill Shepherd and Dan Dent credit for operating with remarkable subtlety, but I can still feel them watching my every move like a hawk. I feel pressure, too, but not because of my investment team partners or anyone else in the firm.

The pressure I feel comes from within, because I've got some lofty performance standards of my own to meet, and also because I feel like my family's future is riding on how well I do during my tenure at T. Rowe Price.

Thankfully, my transition into T. Rowe Price comes along quite smoothly. Thanks to having been here three times prior to starting work, I've entered with a pretty accurate sense of what the portfolio manager job is all about. Things are unfolding just as I anticipated they would, I'm pleased to note.

If you've ever seen the movie *Red October*, or read the book by Tom Clancy, then you're aware that U.S. submarine officers don't have the ability to independently launch nuclear weapons. Instead there's a system of checks and balances that calls for submariners to work together before they can unleash their nukes.

At T. Rowe Price, making investment decisions is the same way. None of the portfolio managers within the teams can be a reckless cowboy and launch an investment independently of his team members. Tons of collaboration is encouraged before the investment trigger can be pulled, so to speak.

To take my military analogy a step further, the ammunition portfolio managers need to do the best possible job is information. So the
various investment teams regularly have inter-team meetings, and also
meet with Price's research analysts at least once a week. That way
the analysts can give us their two cents regarding which companies
they think we may want to add to an approved list of companies we
use for assembling portfolios.

But the most critical bit of information at our disposal is the goals
and objectives and idiosyncrasies of our clients. Basically, my job is to
build mosaics of information and knowledge, while tailoring those
mosaics to particular client needs.

Bill and Dan are beginning to introduce me to some of the clients
that I'll be responsible for. Just as T. Rowe Price has only one African-
American portfolio manager—me, it only has one African-American
client, businessman Henry Parks. Instead of feeling somewhat mortified
about that state of affairs, T. Rowe Price is quite proud of having Parks
in the fold, and even mentioned him to me when I was interviewing!

Whenever I meet clients for the first time, I'm always accompanied by the person who had been working with those clients prior
to my arrival. Not once do I get a raised eyebrow or a funny look—
apparently everyone has been warned beforehand that you're about
to meet T. Rowe Price's first black portfolio manager.

Actually, getting out and meeting clients is proving to be a useful
exercise, after three years of working at a firm where the investing
goals of one family were all I had to worry about. T. Rowe Price's
clients have different risk tolerances, so I can't take a cookie-cutter
approach to what types of investments go into various portfolios.

During my second week with the firm I'm sitting at my desk
looking over some corporate research when the phone rings. On the
other end of the line is local African-American powerhouse Judge
William H. Murphy, Sr., who's with the Maryland District Court.
The patriarch of a well-known political family in Maryland circles,
Judge Murphy wants to know if I would join him for lunch!

When I show up at the appointed place, a popular drugstore in
downtown Baltimore, Judge Murphy is already waiting for me at the
lunch counter. Bald, avuncular, and bespectacled, Judge Murphy carefully looks me up and down before speaking.

"I feel like I know you!" he says with a grin. "I'm really happy to meet you. I know all about you!"

I have no earthly idea what this distinguished looking black gentleman is talking about, and briefly wonder if I'm going to regret not having eaten lunch at my desk while happily poring over market research.

"It's a pleasure meeting you, your honor," I reply, "Sir, what do you mean that 'you know all about me?'"

Finally taking note of my befuddlement Judge Murphy, who's in his late fifties, gently places a hand on my shoulder. "I'm sorry young man," he laughs. "T. Rowe Price is a friend of mine. He's been talking to me for a long time about how his people have been chasing a very bright, talented African American he hoped would join the firm. I had lunch with him several times while you were being considered for the position you just took!"

Judge Murphy stands at the lunch counter for a moment and beams mightily, clearly bursting with pride over my trailblazing achievement at the internationally known investment house headquartered in Baltimore. "If there's anything I can ever do for you, you just let me know," he says.

Wow! If I'm ever on trial within the Maryland District Court system, God forbid, I know which black-robed jurist I'll pray to see!

The funny thing was that Price had retired from his eponymous firm two years prior to my hiring, but clearly has remained extremely plugged in to what's going on. I'm humbled that an icon of investing had such an avid interest in luring me to his firm. I'm also humbled that Judge Murphy personally sought me out to inform me of this.

Chapter 13

Swimming with Sharks

The leader of my three-man team portfolio manager team, Bill Shepherd, has disappeared without explanation, to the shock and consternation of Dan Dent and I.

Two days ago Bill failed to report to work without calling, which is incredibly out of character for an even-keeled rock like Bill. His wife doesn't have a clue about her husband's whereabouts, and now law enforcement officials have launched a full-scale investigation.

The fact that he may be a victim of foul play has cast a pall over all of T. Rowe Price, but especially among the firm's portfolio managers, who are a close-knit tribe. Not surprisingly, professorial Dan Dent is tremendously shaken, because his relationship with Bill goes back a lot further than mine.

I feel sorry for Dan, who often appears to be going through the motions, but I occasionally catch my focus wandering, too. If you work shoulder-to-shoulder with someone and he suddenly vanishes in a suspicious manner that even his spouse can't explain, I guarantee you'll find that development terrifically unsettling. This is true even if you don't particularly care for the missing person, and I happen to like and respect Bill.

If you recall, Sylvia and I went to dinner with Bill, Dan, and their wives while T. Rowe Price was wooing me to join the firm, so this tragedy is hitting Sylvia and I where we live. We've even contacted Bill's spouse to offer encouragement and whatever assistance we can make available, and have prayed for his safety. However, with each passing hour the unthinkable looks more and more likely.

The optimist in me wants to believe Bill is okay, while my realist is coming to grips with the increasing likelihood that he's dead.

That's all but a certainty after months go by without word from Bill. With heavy hearts, Dan and I begin dividing up Bill's clients and getting in contact with them. Whatever misfortune has befallen Bill, life goes on and T. Rowe Price's clients will still have to be accorded the superb, attentive service they've come to expect.

No grief counselors will be made available to T. Rowe Price's staff, because that workplace innovation has yet to be invented. So we all deal with whatever bereavement issues we may be feeling the old-fashioned way—by sucking it up and handling it as best we can.

Months after Bill Shepherd's vanishing act, Dan and I are stunned to be informed that Bill is alive, is out of the country and is deeply entangled in an asset dispute involving a wife Bill had prior to marrying the one Sylvia and I know!

It seems that Bill used the expertise he gained at T. Rowe Price to do exactly what I plan to do—generate impressive personal wealth. But as he was doing this, there was one minor detail that Bill neglected to inform his wife of—Bill was already married and hadn't gotten a divorce when he met her!

After he became rich his first wife came after him, looking for her cut. Bill's solution was to quietly transfer all of his assets to his second wife and then leave the country. Me and everyone else at T. Rowe Price were fearing that Bill might be deceased, when he was actually a bigamist playing an elaborate shell game.

But the last laugh is on him, because after he disappears his second wife divorces him—and keeps his fortune!

The irony, of course, is that despite the boatload of trouble that T. Rowe Price and other investment firms go through to vet people and probe into their backgrounds, every now and then a joker manages to slip into the deck. Years later it would even happen to me after I started my business, despite having one of the more stringent screenings processes imaginable.

Needless to say, Bill's career with T. Rowe Price has come to a spectacular and unceremonious end. The result is that Dan Dent and I now find ourselves a team of two, precisely the situation Dan was in when the firm was looking to hire me.

★ ★ ★

A typical day at work for me now is a fairly helter-skelter, action-packed affair, a most unexpected development for me. Prior to joining T. Rowe Price I thought I was going to have a lot of time for looking over corporate research, allowing me to make investments in a very thoughtful way.

My workload gets even heavier when someone gets wind of the fact that I know a fair amount about fixed-income securities. That's a skill none of the other equity managers possess, so I'm asked to work on the investment committee of T. Rowe Price's bond fund. The investment committee basically runs the bond fund, so I'm learning a lot about fixed-income securities, knowledge that I'll put to very good use later.

If this sounds arduous or taxing, nothing could be further from the truth. I love all of the investment work I'm doing, and would do it for free, truth be told. It's fascinating, rewarding and fulfilling, and I often find that I have to make myself leave T. Rowe Price's offices at the end of the day.

You'll find me already at my desk at eight in the morning and I usually leave around seven in the evening. So for me, a 10-hour day is a short one. Also, like most people involved in investing at a serious level, I put in another hour or so of reading after the girls have been tucked into bed.

It's a good thing that I find my profession enthralling, because the stock market has been in serious decline through 1973 and 1974. I'm getting an awful lot of practice performing the most difficult task in the investment business—telling investors that their stocks are underperforming, while simultaneously trying to convince them not to pull out of the market.

I now have responsibility for a fair number of major institutional funds, and telling investment committee members that their T. Rowe Price positions are performing poorly is difficult as heck. That's because the committee members are getting a lot of sideways glances back at the companies, foundations, funds, and universities they work for, and are taking heat. And as everyone knows, to paraphrase an earthy popular saying, heat always seems to flow downhill.

When I'm being grilled by investment committee members of pension funds, endowment funds, and foundations whose stocks aren't performing as expected, the committee members tend to hold my feet to the fire relative to a common market benchmark.

For mid-cap portfolios, for example, the Russell Midcap Growth Index is the generally accepted benchmark. For portfolios investing in smaller companies, the Russell 2000 Growth Index is generally considered the accepted standard.

On the other hand, the Dow Jones Industrial Average isn't generally used as a yardstick by institutional investors, because it only covers 30 companies. The Standard & Poor's 500 is generally a widely accepted benchmark for the market as a whole.

So agitated investment committee members love nothing more than to pepper you with indignant, and at times insolent, questions when their performance is barely exceeding, or falling below, the numbers displayed by these various indexes.

I don't particularly like facing angry clients, but it's not a responsibility I duck, either. First of all, I'm an investor myself and I know what it feels like to back a stock with my hard-earned money and watch it underperform. Fortunately, it's not something that happens to me often.

I don't take angry clients personally and I don't try to sugarcoat or downplay their losses. Once they've had an opportunity to vent, I explain to them that at T. Rowe Price, the emphasis is on a long-term investing approach. I then reassure clients that the stocks we've purchased are in companies that embrace great business models and that have stellar management.

The market at a given point in time may not recognize all of the attributes that we at T. Rowe Price see as investors, I tell antsy clients over and over when I talk to them about the stock market's doldrums. And I end by noting that if they simply hold their positions and resist the temptation to get cold feet, they'll likely wind up in a better position over time.

This isn't some canned spiel on my part, either—this is what I truly believe. And underlying those words is a confidence that what I'm saying and doing is the right way to go.

I remember giving what I felt was a brilliant presentation to an investment committee for Illinois Bell during the down market. Afterward, an old codger on the committee fixed me with a piercing stare and simply said: "You can gold-plate it, young man, but a turd is still a turd!"

Boy, talk about kicking the wind out of your sails!

As harsh as that may sound, institutions are generally far more understanding about market fluctuations than wealthy investors tend to be. That's because institutional investors usually embrace a long-term orientation to investing, and appreciate that stocks are cyclical in nature. Plus, institutional investors are prone to judge their performance relative to the appropriate index.

Wealthy investors, on the other hand, often want to do better than the market when it's going up, but don't want to lose money when it's going down. They typically want to have it both ways, and frequently have to be educated that this just isn't possible.

All in all, getting involved with the care and feeding of investment clients is proving to be an invaluable experience. I'm learning that if I'm truthful, confront bad news directly, and base my presentations on facts, clients tend to appreciate that. I'm also finding that it's very important to keep believing in my investment strategies and to not deviate from them even during tough times.

You can be the most brilliant stock picker who ever lived, but if you can't bedazzle clients with stellar people skills, it's difficult—if not impossible—to do well as an equity manager at T. Rowe Price. I also need to become a rainmaker capable of drawing business to the firm, something I'm working at by constantly broadening my circle of business contacts.

Two years after I join T. Rowe Price, Dan Dent leaves to start his own investment counseling firm, making me the only surviving member on what had been a three-man investment team. You'd think the firm's turnover rate might be incredibly high the way things have played out in the short time I've been here, but that's really not the case.

So a decision is made to place me on an investment team that has the most portfolio managers, as well as the most assets. I'm bringing a number of very large accounts with me, and quickly learn that the collegiality and bonhomie I've observed at T. Rowe Price thus far can evaporate at a moment's notice.

The more assets you have under your wing at Price, the higher your perceived importance and value within the firm. The large accounts I'm toting around are each worth hundreds of millions of dollars and have drawn the unwanted attention of Kyle Daniels, a very senior and highly respected colleague. A member of the large team I'm transitioning to, Kyle wants my accounts for himself and has devised a plan to take them from me.

I'm hearing through the grapevine that Kyle has been telling the two leaders of my new team that my large accounts are at risk with me, because I'm too new to the way things are done at T. Rowe Price.

Where does Kyle think my multi-million dollar accounts would be safest? With him, of course, under the rationale that's he's an old hand and knows best how to properly service them!

Call me naïve, but I really am kind of taken aback and perplexed at this kind of back-alley, brass-knuckle behavior. But at the same time, I have absolutely no intention of meekly surrendering my accounts to Kyle without a fight. I just have to defend myself in a way that doesn't make waves, because I don't want to jeopardize my standing at the firm.

I may be soft-spoken and polite to a fault, but I'm nobody's patsy. And I'll be darned if Kyle is going to roll in here like some obnoxious schoolyard bully and shake me down for hundreds of millions of dollars worth of my lunch money.

So I'm pretty annoyed as I sit in my small office on T. Rowe Price's third floor, strategizing on how to best deal with Kyle and his chicanery. It's late in the afternoon and the time I'm devoting to neutralizing his unscrupulous behavior could be better utilized by going over materials related to corporate research. If I've gotten wind of Kyle's unethical power play, I'm sure a lot of other portfolio managers know about it, too.

Who might be a potential ally within the new investment team I'm moving into? I need someone who's credible and who has an inherent sense of fairness.

The name that keeps popping into my head is Bob Hall. A T. Rowe Price employee since 1966 and seven years older than I am, Bob is a total class act, is wise, and has a terrific sense of humor. Plus, I've seen no evidence he might be part of a cabal that includes Kyle.

Gathering some materials from my desk, I walk down the hall to Bob's office, ostensibly to talk about work. When I stroll through his doorway, he doesn't seem at all surprised to see me.

"How are ya, Ed?" Bob asks with what I would almost swear is a knowing smile. "What's shaking?"

I ask him a few questions about an investing issue that was discussed earlier during a research meeting, before segueing into the real reason I dropped by. "Bob," I say, seeing to it that my voice and expression remain totally neutral, "how well do you know Kyle Daniels?"

Bob doesn't answer immediately. Instead, he gets up from his desk and starts rummaging through some financial magazines stacked atop his bookcase. "I've been here a decade now," he says finally, as he pulls a magazine off the shelf and idly flips it. "I know Kyle's M.O. pretty doggone well. Can you excuse me for a moment?"

Before I can answer Bob mysteriously leaves me sitting in his office as he ambles out the door, magazine in hand. He returns a few minutes later and hands me four photocopied pages of a magazine article. The piece is titled "Swimming With Sharks" and it's about a businessman whose behavior is decidedly shady in terms of what he'll do to gain a competitive advantage.

What Bob is basically telling me is: "You don't realize it, whippersnapper, but Kyle Daniels is a great white shark of the first order. You're no longer in the tranquil, gentile investment wading pool that was Irwin Management Co. Better practice your breast stroke and grab some shark repellent. Might want to watch your back, too!"

A smile slowly creases my face as I read the first few paragraphs of Bob's article. Without uttering a single incriminating word, he's told me everything I need to know. Both about himself and Kyle. Thanks for the warning, because in the two and a half years that I've been swimming in the deep waters of T. Rowe Price, none of the sharks has bared their teeth.

Silly me—here I was thinking we were all working in concert to maximum value for our clients! And double shame on me, because I actually believed we were all seeking to do that through hard work and ethical behavior.

Fortunately, Kyle's back-stabbing gambit is dismissed out of hand by my team leaders, as it should be. Bob is appointed to help me handle some of my large accounts, beginning a very close friendship and working relationship that would continue into the next millennium.

As for Kyle, our relationship moving forward is best described as cordial, and very, very cool. I keep my distance from him during the remainder of my time at T. Rowe Price. There are two kinds of people that really rub me the wrong way, with deceitful folks heading the list. I also don't have much patience with those who are always boasting about themselves.

Frankly, I'm surprised at the manner in which he underestimated me.

Bob and I go on to manage some of the largest institutional clients T. Rowe Price has, to Kyle's everlasting chagrin.

Due to the fact that it takes until 1977 for growth stocks to rebound appreciably, much of our time is spent on the road taking verbal beatings from clients. Bob and I have gotten awfully good at explaining and justifying, as well as at letting rude and intemperate comments roll off our backs.

One of T. Rowe Price's very biggest accounts is Southern New England Telephone, which Bob and I are responsible for. One winter night when it's snowing like heck, the two of us have to fly to New Haven, Connecticut, for a meeting with Southern New England Telephone's investment committee.

As we're waiting inside Philadelphia International Airport for a connecting flight to New Haven, a little single-engine propeller plane comes whirring up to the terminal, it's landing lights illuminating big fat flakes of snow that look to be the size of Frisbees. Being deathly afraid of blizzards and one-engine airplanes, Bob has just about turned green.

"Eddie," Bob intones, his eyes growing wider by the second, "that's our plane. And we're not getting on it!"

I have no more desire to board that rickety-looking puddle jumper in the middle of a driving snowstorm than Bob does. In fact, I'm appalled that a commuter airline would present us with such an inherently unsafe proposition. But just to get a rise out of Bob, I make believe I'm anxious to risk death and fly on that ridiculous thing, so we can make our Southern New England Telephone meeting!

We laugh about that episode all the time as we catch planes crisscrossing the United States, including red-eye flights back from the West Coast. You really get to know a person when you travel with them on a regular basis, and Bob and I have formed a terrifically tight bond.

Some clients require us to attend meetings quarterly, while for others twice a year is sufficient. I'm living out of my suitcase so much that I vow that if I ever start my own investment firm, I'll tell my clients that quarterly meetings are wasteful and that annual meetings are better. I say this because when you're devoting a lot of effort to maintaining face time with a client four times a year, much of that time would be better spent by having your investment manager stay at the office and look for ways to improve your portfolio.

Every day that I come to work at T. Rowe Price, I'm "stealing knowledge" as the saying goes. I learn something fascinating about the world of investing on a daily basis, and thanks to my base salary and annual bonuses, my remuneration is quite impressive . . . but I'm still just an employee.

Despite my Brooks Brothers suits and wing-tipped shoes, I'm an entrepreneur at heart. Regardless of how cushy and comfortable my velvet handcuffs grow, I'm proud to note that the restless, entrepreneurial side of my personality refuses to be tamped down, refuses to be bought off.

Uncle Jake would get a kick out of that.

Chapter 14

Aren't You
That Financial Guy
From TV?

At long last, a return to normalcy.

After performing cantankerously much of 1973, 1974, 1975, and 1976, growth stocks finally start getting their luster back in 1977.

I've been at T. Rowe Price four years now, and in that time have earned a Ph.D. in terms of my ability to assuage the fears of surly, impatient clients who are sick and doggone tired of lagging the market. I don't blame them, either.

The four years have sharply honed my portfolio-management skills, in terms of making judgments about which companies might make decent long-term investments.

Portfolio management is all about understanding your clients' needs, then fashioning a portfolio from available investment opportunities that dovetail with their style of investing.

I've done well, well enough to have been offered T. Rowe Price stock at a very reasonable price, making me an equity owner in the company. Stock is only offered to management members viewed as valued team members. That stock will wind up playing a very significant role in my future.

I have T. Rowe Price Jr. to thank for this. He held that the most important assets of a service organization are its people, and recognized that they walk out the door every night.

So in order to protect those valuable assets he believed it was imperative to:

- Treat people well as human beings
- Compensate them very well
- Offer them a piece of the pie in terms of ownership in the firm
- Give them a pleasant work environment

Price felt that if those things are taken care of, then people will tend to stay and continue to be productive. Therefore, equity ownership was one of his fundamental retention tools.

I will wind up borrowing all four of his retention tenets after starting Brown Capital Management.

Getting back to giving employees the opportunity to purchase stock, Price also felt that it was important for active employees to be shareholders. So if anyone leaves T. Rowe Price for any reason— resignation, death, retirement, termination—their stock has to be sold back within five years.

I want to mention one other investment opportunity at the firm that benefitted me greatly. It will become apparent later why these investments are significant.

The second windfall resulted from an endeavor Mr. Price started along with a former T. Rowe Price manager. It was known as New Enterprise Associates (NEA) and T. Rowe Price gave shareholders a percentage of an NEA venture capital partnership, Pratt Street Ventures, that was pro-rated according to how much T. Rowe Price stock you owned.

Things worked out in a way that enabled me to retain holdings in both my T. Rowe Price stock and in the partnership interests, a situation that continues to benefit my family and I financially to this very day.

I had anticipated this kind of thing when I left IBM to get my MBA, and also when I subsequently went to Irwin Management and then T. Rowe Price. One thing I hadn't foreseen about the move to T. Rowe Price, though, is becoming a national TV personality.

Just about everyone in the investment industry tunes in to watch a weekly PBS program called "Wall $treet Week With Louis Rukeyser," which has between five million and six million viewers. Every Friday evening Sylvia and I camp out on the couch in our living room and watch "Wall $treet Week," which is broadcast live. It's been on the air for eight years now, and only one T. Rowe Price financial expert has been featured thus far.

A tall, white-haired, droll man who's never encountered a pun he didn't like, Lou is a journalist who at various points was a foreign and financial correspondent with the *Baltimore Sun*, an economics correspondent and commentator with ABC TV, and a syndicated newspaper columnist. Through hard work and savvy self promotion, he's managed to parlay his journalism background into being a respected and nationally known financial pundit with a loyal following among television, radio, print, and live audiences.

"Wall $treet Week" is produced by Maryland Public Television in Owings Mills, Maryland, a few miles north of Baltimore. After kicking off every show with a monologue pegged to a topical financial market development, Lou presides over a roundtable with three financial specialists who are regulars on his program. Lou does his next segment from a couch, where he interviews special guests.

Such is Lou's influence that when a company is highlighted on his Friday evening show, it often results in a spurt in the firm's stock on Monday. Likewise, financial experts who manage to appear on Lou's program experience an upsurge in recognition. Being asked to be on "Wall $treet Week With Louis Rukeyser" is a very big deal!

Now that growth stocks are reestablishing themselves as darlings of the investment world, the producers of "Wall $treet Week" need a growth-stock portfolio expert. And in a nod to the startling lack of diversity usually seen on the show, the hunt is on for an African-American growth-stock portfolio manager.

It seems the only person fitting that description nationwide is yours truly, so I'm approached by one of my two team leaders and asked if I'll consider doing a segment on Lou's show. It takes me about three-tenths of a second to answer in the affirmative. Man oh man oh man! How often does a fat plum like this drop in your lap?

All portfolio managers want to attract more business to their firms, and I can't think of a better way to get T. Rowe Price's, and Ed Brown's names out there.

Seconds before the TV camera comes on, I find myself sitting in a Maryland Public Television studio across from Louis Rukeyser, with my makeup neatly applied, my Afro perfectly coifed and feeling nervous as heck. I'm not going to lie. I take a deep breath and for a split second don't think about growth stocks, Lou's millions of viewers, and the fact that my wife and two daughters are anxiously staring at the TV in the living room, practically willing Daddy not to screw up on L-I-V-E television.

Instead I visualize the calming visage of Grandma, and imagine that she's sitting somewhere with Lady B., and they're both proudly exhorting me on. That wonderful mental picture has the desired calming effect. Then I think back to a bit of advice one of Lou's nice producers offered in the greenroom as I was getting made up—simply make believe that Lou and I are having a leisurely one-on-one discussion about one of my favorite topics on the entire planet: growth stocks.

When it comes to questions mailed into "Wall $treet Week With Louis Rukeyser" by viewers, panelists on the show know beforehand what those queries are going to be. However, no one ever has any inkling what Lou might toss out once the red light on the studio TV camera blinks on. I don't consider this a problem, because I could literally hold forth on growth stocks for hours on end if I could get away with it.

The segment with Lou goes swimmingly. I smoothly cover all of my talking points and I hear myself casually telling Lou "thank you for having me on the program" preparatory to leaving the set.

Being someone who studiously avoids the spotlight and who abhors people who draw attention to themselves, I'm surprised at how thoroughly and comprehensively I'm enjoying my 15 minutes of fame following my "Wall $treet Week With Louis Rukeyser" cameo. The glad-handing at T. Rowe Price has been going on for two days nonstop, and the way that Kyle Daniels looks as though he could strangle me is absolutely priceless.

The pride in the eyes of the handful of other African Americans working at Price gives me goose bumps, and it's been amazing to have complete strangers stop me in downtown Baltimore during my lunch break to congratulate me.

But by far the best "Wall $treet Week With Louis Rukeyser" perk has been the way my family has been gazing at me with something akin to adoration. That may not last long, but it sure feels pretty darned spectacular while it does. "Wall $treet Week" has given me a boost with clients, too. That was my main objective starting out, but it's become secondary when contrasted to the gazes of admiration I'm getting from Sylvia, Tonya, and Jennifer.

But in time the acclaim and buzz die down, as they invariably do, and it's back to the business of giving T. Rowe Price's growth-stock clients exemplary service, while luring new ones into the fold. Despite all the fancy graphs and pie charts and impressive-sounding nomenclature associated with investing, at its core it's a pretty simple game— make people happy by making them money, and always keep the circle of smiling, affluent faces constantly growing.

I believe I've gotten to be pretty proficient at that over the course of eight years in the money management business.

A few months after my appearance on "Wall $treet Week With Louis Rukeyser," one of his producers calls me at home out of the blue. "You really did a nice job when you came on the show back in September," he notes, before knocking me off my feet. "Lou wants to know if you'd like to be one of his regular rotating panelists?"

Wow!

I've just been handed a national platform to hold forth on the world of growth-stock investing, on the financial program with the largest viewership in the United States. "Wall $treet Week With Louis Rukeyser" makes me a nationally known financial pundit, never a bad thing when your aim is to be a rainmaker and noted investor.

Bob Hall and I can be in Albuquerque or Minneapolis or Seattle for a client meeting and someone will invariably approach and shake my hand and tell me they saw me on Lou Rukeyser's show. They usually ask me for a stock tip, too, which I politely decline.

First of all, would you go up to an attorney and ask for free legal advice? But second, I don't want to recommend a stock and then not have it perform well, especially if I'm not around to suggest that it may be time to sell. Not only would I feel horrible about that, but I'm sure someone might eventually get the bright idea to sue me.

Still, I thoroughly enjoy the business advantage that "Wall $treet Week" gives me. Instead of being just another top-notch T. Rowe Price portfolio manager, I'm the guy that a potential client likely saw talking about financial matters on national TV. In our celebrity crazy society, the show gives me a slight leg up that I gladly accept.

I get the ball rolling on my rotating panelist gig in May 1979. Another perk associated with "Wall $treet Week" is that a dinner is always held for panelists and guests, allowing me to meet some of the heaviest hitters in economics and finance.

Along with asking for stock tips, strangers always want to know what Lou Rukeyser is like? For starters he's Jewish, which gives him a certain sensitivity to inclusion and diversity. Lou is keenly aware that Wall Street's high-powered jobs are overwhelmingly held by white males, and has gone out of his way to include female and African-American panelists on "Wall $treet Week With Louis Rukeyser."

Some people have a natural presence about them, and Lou is one of those individuals. A tall, well-dressed man, Lou loves to talk about his finely honed sartorial tastes. Despite the fact that he's on television every week, I've never seen him don the same exquisitely tailored suit twice.

A bit of a character, Lou wants to eventually enjoy a meal in each of France's five-star Michelin restaurants. One time after I alert him that I'm about to head to France on a family vacation, Lou makes it a point to pull me aside in order to recommend restaurants that I may want to visit. Sure enough, the cuisine in each is downright memorable.

Tremendously effusive when clothes, fine French dining, or economics are the topic of discussion, Lou isn't a particularly warm individual otherwise. The two of us get along well, and have even gone to dinner several times, but our relationship is more professional than buddy-buddy. His natural inclination is to let you know him up to a point, and then hold you at arm's length.

Still, I'm fond of Lou and greatly admire the way that a man who is basically a journalist has been able to transform himself into a one-man cottage industry when it comes to financial information. Lou is remunerated very handsomely for giving speeches, and attracts tens of thousands of people to his financial seminars. Plus he pens a respected, syndicated financial column that appears in newspapers nationwide and publishes two profitable newsletters.

In light of the fact that his journalistic career started with the *Baltimore Sun*, and the fact that "Wall $treet Week With Louis Rukeyser" originates from a studio in suburban Baltimore, it baffles and galls Lou to no end that none of Baltimore's three major papers carry his syndicated financial column. He's not at all shy about articulating his befuddlement and irritation over what he views as an inexcusable, unforgiveable slight.

Needless to say, it's practically impossible to accomplish what Lou has without possessing an outsized ego. His is quite healthy, so it's understood on the "Wall $treet Week With Louis Rukeyser" set that it's Lou's show.

He prefers that all financial pearls of wisdom from guests and panelists be dispensed inside of 40 seconds. If I give a particularly impassioned response to a question, Lou is likely to pull me aside after the show and say: "Ed, you went a minute and five seconds. Let's work on that next time!"

Another edict of Lou's, and one that makes perfect sense to me, is that "Wall $treet Week With Louis Rukeyser" has an ironclad ban on financial industry jargon. Any time a financial expert starts spouting arcane, inside-baseball terms that laymen won't understand, Lou's standard response is: "Could you please explain that to me in English?"

Finally, panelists and guests on the show should never advance arguments or make suggestions that contradict Lou, or otherwise make him appear stupid!

Heck, I can abide by those house rules. "Wall $treet Week With Louis Rukeyser" presents me with millions of dollars worth of free, coast-to-coast publicity for pushing the Ed Brown brand, so trampling Lou's toes is the absolute furthest thing from my mind.

After only a year as a regular on Lou's weekly show, I notice a definite difference in the way I'm perceived inside and outside T. Rowe Price. Inside the firm, the biggest difference is the good-natured zingers Bob tosses my way about being a media star. Outside,

I'm finding that a lot of people—both financial industry insiders and ordinary citizens—know who I am.

I didn't get into the money management business, or join T. Rowe Price, to become a celebrity among the financial cognoscenti, but to my bemusement that's exactly what's happened.

Being a "Wall $treet Week" regular has made it easier for me to nab large institutional clients in some instances. For example, if I'm competing with a portfolio manager from another firm, and we're pretty much running neck-and-neck, being a nationally recognized financial pundit often tips the scales in my favor.

Of course once I attract new business to T. Rowe Price, nobody gives a darn about my talking-head achievements. Once onboard, all a client wants to see is sterling portfolio performance, and fortunately I've been able to outperform the benchmark stock market indexes on a fairly consistent basis over the long term.

But clearly "Wall $treet Week" has nicely augmented the skill, dedication, and hard work I bring to the art of stock picking, and I'm grateful to Lou and to his show, which ran on Maryland Public Television for 32 years. He left Maryland Public Television in a snit in 2002, after its management made a curious decision to dramatically throttle back Lou's involvement with "Wall $treet Week" to five-minute segments.

Lou started another financial program on CNBC, but ended it in 2003 due to declining health and he passed away from bone cancer at his Connecticut home in 2006.

Shortly after his death, one of his daughters calls to inform me that her father knew his demise was imminent, so he took the trouble of planning his own memorial service. Lou has arranged for it to take place at the Lincoln Center for the Performing Arts, in Manhattan, and has even drawn up a guest list of 400 people.

I can't help but smile as I listen—from beyond the grave, Lou is still adroitly running the show with the firmest of hands.

He's decreed that his memorial service not last more than one hour and fifteen minutes, and has asked that five of the 23 people who served as panelists on his show over the years speak at his memorial service. I'm flabbergasted when Lou's daughter tells me that her father picked me to be one of the five!

"He thought the world of you and always talked about you," she says.

"Really?" I reply, feeling genuinely touched. "I never knew that!" But thinking back on it, Lou dropped a not-so-subtle hint by inducting me into the Louis Rukeyser Wall $treet Week Hall of Fame in 1996. I merely attributed that to my expertise in the area of growth stocks.

I never surmised there might be a personal component attached to the honor.

On the date of Lou's memorial service, I drive to New York City and speak from the heart about one of the most magnetic, fascinating, and enigmatic individuals I've ever encountered. And I do so within a strictly enforced five-minute time frame—per Lou's instructions.

Without question, Louis Richard Rukeyser was a visionary in terms of appreciating that the investing public is hungry for thought-provoking, solid financial discourse and dialogue. Basically, there was no place where you could consistently get that kind of thing prior to Lou, and I really don't think there has been since.

Chapter 15

Walking a
Racial Tightrope

By now it's clear that I'm an African American who regularly engages in pursuits conventional wisdom says aren't "black." Like sending my girls to predominantly white private schools in Baltimore.

And flying airplanes. And managing investment portfolios worth tens of millions of dollars.

The *Washington Post* has picked up on this, too. I'm not sure how they got my name, but they approach me in 1978 about participating in a piece whose basic theme is "staying black in a white world." I'm initially bemused after a *Post* reporter asks if I would mind being interviewed. But after thinking about it a bit, long before this country's love affair with Cliff and Claire Huxtable plays out on TV, I come to the conclusion that the *Post's* premise has merit and is worth examining.

I bounce the idea off Sylvia, because she and I routinely make a concerted effort to raise our daughters—who are now 12 and nine—with a sense of racial pride. We want them to be firmly in touch with

African-American culture and sensibilities, even though they're frequently in settings that couldn't be less "black."

A mere decade after the assassination of Martin Luther King, my wife and I aren't about to try to sell our kids some fairy tale about living in a kumbaya, post-racial society. That would be irresponsible.

So after a brief conversation out of the girls' earshot, Sylvia and I agree that we're in—we're going to do the article. As a courtesy, I let my supervisors at T. Rowe Price know that I'm going to be featured in a *Washington Post* article focusing on race.

And then Sylvia, Tonya, Jennifer, and I allow the same newspaper that broke Watergate to take detailed snapshots of our lives. My primary concern is that the story be executed in a way that's nuanced and accurate, and without making my family or I look like a quartet of African-American ninnies.

If you've never been a reporter's quarry, I assure you that it's one of the most helpless feelings in the world. Because regardless of what slant or spin you may hope to put on things, irrespective of how nice you may have been to that journalist, once he or she gathers up their tape recorder and notepad and leaves, the tenor of the ensuing article rests totally in the hands of that individual, and his or her editors.

If the reporter has an ax to grind, a preconceived bias in search of substantiation, or just happens to be a sloppy fact-gatherer, the result can be downright mortifying for whoever is being written about.

When the story finally appears, it's on the day of heaviest newspaper readership, Sunday, and is on the front page of the *Washington Post*. The lengthy article delves into the lives of five regional African-American couples who are plying trades viewed as nontraditional for African Americans.

Among the various couples, the breadwinners are all well-compensated, pursue fields that call for graduate degrees, are the only black person in their workplaces, and all live in well-to-do neighborhoods that are mostly white.

Sensitively written and nicely packaged, the story chronicles how Sylvia and I have joined an African-American travel group in the Baltimore area known as the Black Hawks. Basically, the Black Hawks are 12 couples who have children and who all own road-going RVs. One weekend a month, except during the winter, the Black Hawks target a campground within a three-hour radius of Baltimore, and then we collectively hit the road for a camping weekend with our families.

The *Washington Post* also tells its readers how Sylvia and I go out of our way to ensure that our daughters have some black playmates to cavort with, and how even though the two of us have joined a predominantly white Presbyterian church in Baltimore, we make it a point to take the girls to a black church at least one Sunday per month.

The underlying point, for Sylvia and I at least, is that we want Tonya and Jennifer to move with ease and total self assurance between the black and white worlds. But even more importantly, we want them to understand that they're members of a group that's always made invaluable contributions to this country, despite anything they may hear to the contrary.

My wife and I never want blackness to be an abstraction to our children, and want them to always comprehend the full measure of the struggles, challenges, and triumphs African Americans have experienced on these shores.

Both Sylvia and I have seen instances where affluent African Americans have allowed their children to naively operate as if the United States were a homogenous, color-blind meritocracy, and the children happen to be no different than anyone else.

When these kids have their inevitable day of reckoning, it's always an experience that leaves shock, disillusionment, and bitterness in its wake. That stems from irresponsible and lazy parenting, in my estimation. Shaping and guiding the socialization of black children used to affluent, mostly white environments calls for extra work that some parents aren't willing to do.

Sylvia and I will do whatever is necessary to ensure that Tonya's and Jennifer's internal compasses are properly aligned when it comes to their African-American roots. This may strike some as exotica, but to my spouse and I, it's just the day-to-day reality of life in the Brown household.

However, if the *Washington Post* piece manages to open some eyes, that's a good thing. A few of my all-white colleagues on T. Rowe Price's equity management team candidly tell me that they never thought about the duality of my existence prior to reading the article. Truth be told, I don't think about it much either, just as people who speak more than one language fluently just do it reflexively.

By the way, even though the *Post* article is only tangentially related to business, I took its potential impact on my work into account. Therefore, I'm pleased to note that the piece makes mention of the fact that I'm a portfolio manager for T. Rowe Price.

When I can discuss a noteworthy social phenomenon in the press, and get free publicity, it doesn't get much better than that.

To finish out the topic of race and business, the paucity of African Americans working as professionals inside investment houses is downright alarming to me. Equally alarming is the plethora of lame excuses typically mouthed to justify this state of affairs. Number one on the list has to be "we just can't find anybody with the talent we're looking for!"

I've always made a concerted effort to find African Americans with experience in the investment business, and I've never had any problem. All you need to have is the will.

Chapter 16

"Go For It, Dad!"

Will the last portfolio manager to exit T. Rowe Price please turn off the lights!

That may be a bit of an exaggeration, but it is true that an awful lot of my colleagues walked out the door in 1981 and 1982. And truth be told, I really don't think I'm that far behind them.

My contemporaries are bidding T. Rowe Price adieu to start financial firms of their own. What they're doing has been in the back of my mind from the day I started. But during my ninth year with the firm, the desire crystallizes into something so strong and undeniable that creating my own business is something I *have* to do.

Nine years as a portfolio manager at one of the best investment firms in the business have taught me most of the lessons I need to know to hang out a shingle and start my own money management firm. I'm now comfortable enough with my abilities to conclude that: *I can definitely do this for myself, and do it well!*

Along the way, I've put a tremendous amount of time and energy into preparing myself for the next step, doing things like earning a

Chartered Financial Analyst (CFA) designation. The tremendously rigorous CFA test—administered by an independent organization—is only given once a year, and has a pass rate of less than 40 percent.

Having a CFA designation says a lot about the person holding it, because the international certification isn't a required credential and it's terrifically difficult to earn. Having those three initials behind your name indicates competence as well as perseverance, because it takes three years to tackle and digest the requisite mountain of financial information you have to master to take the test.

During my tenure at T. Rowe Price, I have also been preparing myself to have an in-depth understanding of the world of philanthropy and how it operates. I don't want to be one of those individuals who parachutes into a philanthropic situation, simply writes a check, and then blithely disappears.

So Sylvia and I have been serving on the boards of charitable organizations that we find worthwhile. For about four years I've been on the board of the Woodburn Center, a residential treatment center serving a predominantly African American clientele. Plus, I recently joined the board of the Baltimore Community Foundation, a philanthropic group seeking to make greater Baltimore a better place to live.

My philanthropic and financial-management ducks are all neatly in a row and exactly where I need them to be at this point in my life. I'm 41 years old and have a total of 12 years of investment-related experience under my belt. This is the perfect time to launch my own investment firm, because I'm still young enough to reenter the work-force without too much difficulty if I happen to crash and burn.

But I have a strong hunch that failure isn't in the cards.

Because along with competence, preparation, and unbridled ambition and optimism, I've got another ace in the hole that tips the scales in my favor. Namely, I've got a big enough nest egg from my investments, savings, and T. Rowe Price stock to keep my family in good financial shape for three years should my company fail to generate a single penny during that time frame.

So I'm not rolling the dice with my family's security if I start my own money management firm. However, if I don't start one, I'll be selling my future—and theirs—short.

What's needed at this point is a sales job, where I sit down with my family and broach the subject of starting a business.

Sylvia, Tonya, Jennifer, and I are arrayed around the dinner table in our house one afternoon, finishing off a leisurely meal, when I clear my throat.

"Everybody, I have something to share with you," I hear myself calmly intoning. "It's something I've been giving an awful lot of thought lately."

I have everybody's undivided attention now. Good. With their expressions ranging from suspicious to indifferent to vaguely alarmed, my three lovely ladies wait to see what the unpredictable head of the Brown household is about to unleash. Well, I'm going to lay a doozy on them.

"I've been at T. Rowe Price for nine years now," I tell my rapt clan. "I have really learned a lot over that time frame, and feel that I've gotten pretty good at what I do. And T. Rowe Price pays me pretty well, too. But I can make a lot more money by creating my own business. So that's exactly what I'm going to do."

I look from one face to the next and for a split second it is deathly quiet in my home, a real rarity. When someone finally says something it's Tonya, who's now 16.

"Oh my god—what about my college education?" my darling daughter blurts out. It's all I can do to keep from bursting into laughter over Tonya's comment, which is uttered with classic teenage self-absorption, angst, and brutal honesty.

"I already planned for that," I reply reassuringly. "I've got enough socked away to keep a roof over our heads and food on the table for three years, if need be. And yes, I even factored in college tuition—unless you had your sights set on Princeton or Yale."

Which I secretly hope she does. I'll delve more into my obsession with Ivy League schools later.

Jennifer, who is 13 and probably the most entrepreneurial of my three audience members, is shooting me a broad smile of admiration and approval.

"Go for it, Dad!" she says succinctly, then rises from the table and gives me a hug, all but assuring that her Christmas wish list is likely to be approved in its entirety later this year.

My two wonderful offspring have weighed in with their impressions of Operation Independence, but the queen of the household is alarmingly subdued and nonverbal. Sylvia will probably feel better after I cross my heart that we absolutely, positively will not have to move from the comfortable home we built in Baltimore County five years ago. And her comfort level will probably shoot up after I sit down with her and painstakingly go over the numbers substantiating the three-year cushion I've been mentioning.

When I share my news with close friends, some of them articulate what Sylvia probably wanted to, but didn't in the interest of maintaining the peace. They tell me that I am absolutely, unequivocally, certifiably nuts to contemplate leaving the safe haven of T. Rowe Price in order to start a business that may or may not succeed. In other words, "How in the world could you wriggle out of those velvet handcuffs, and the fantastic perks and benefits that come with them?"

That's the difference, I guess, between entrepreneurs and those who need the security of a job.

I don't share my plans with anybody at work. The one person I might have confided in has already beaten me to the punch—Bob Hall left with some other Price portfolio managers earlier this year to start their own investment business.

Now that I am absolutely certain my days at T. Rowe Price are numbered, I reach out to a former colleague who's already mastered the path I'm about to tread. Seven years ago, in 1975, David Kirr was an equity manager at Irwin Management Co. who left to co-found Kirr, Marbach & Co., in Columbus, Indiana. Having no desire to waste any time reinventing the wheel, I use Dave as an informational touchstone now that I'm about to leave T. Rowe Price.

Dave's company is still in operation and is prospering, so he must be doing something right. He's also a very gracious individual, and throws himself fully into the role of serving as my entrepreneurial mentor. I'm not at all shy about reaching out to Dave whenever I have a question about something, and I follow his sage advice to the letter.

One of his most valuable insights has to do with the role of support staff in my new business. His philosophy, which I embrace wholly, is that support staff will play a crucial role in determining whether my company succeeds or flops, so Dave recommends hiring the very best support staffers available and compensating them well.

I've heard that philosophy before—from T. Rowe Price.

Another tenet of Dave's that's dead on has to do with clients. Dave's advice is pretty straightforward—never accept a client that I may later regret, just for the sake of having a client. Instead, vet potential clients carefully and with extreme patience, with an eye toward whether the marriage of their investment needs and my financial services will result in a productive and harmonious long-term relationship.

Dave also gives me excellent operational tips, such as securing the services of a top-notch custodian bank and negotiating a lower-than-normal fee in anticipation of large amounts of future business. Having a custodian bank is important because investment managers don't physically take custody of client money or securities.

I've resolved to be principled about my resignation from T. Rowe Price and will not try to take any of its clients with me. Yeah, that ratchets up the degree of difficulty a bit, but that's how confident I am of my ability to grow my own client base. Furthermore, should I have to come back to Price in a few years with my hat in hand, it will definitely be held against me if I tapped into the client base while still working here.

Finally, not trying to take T. Rowe Price's clients is just the right thing to do. The last thing I need to do is start a new money management firm while trying to erase a karmic debt.

In the summer of 1982, I go on vacation for three weeks, the longest I've ever taken. No telling when my next vacation will be once my firm is up and running. So my family and I spend a week in England, a week in France, and a week in Germany. And as a treat to myself, I travel to Mercedes-Benz's headquarters in Stuttgart, Germany, and take delivery on a 1982 Mercedes 240D that I have shipped back to the United States.

Those three weeks in Europe represent the best vacation time I have ever spent. Not necessarily because of the locales, which were nice, but because for the first time I'm able to spend three straight weeks of quality time with my family without business-related intrusions.

As an aside, while in Europe I was approached several times by Americans who amble over to relate that they've seen me on "Wall $treet Week With Louis Rukeyser" and enjoy listening to my stock-picking advice! In addition to giving my ego a little boost, and giving my family something to rib me about, each encounter reaffirms my decision to leave T. Rowe Price and start my own financial business.

How many of my colleagues hanging out shingles get to peri-odically demonstrate their stock-picking prowess on a national television show?

After we return to the States, I start addressing the million and one little details necessary to get an investment firm up and running. Bob Hall helps me find an attorney who has no links to T. Rowe Price, because I still haven't notified my employers that I'm leaving.

I also find an accountant, as well as a custodian bank to deal with client funds. The name of my business is going to be Brown Capital Management. A corporate title doesn't get much more straightforward than that. It gives the name of the firm principal and a pithy explanation of the service being offered.

My bosses at T. Rowe Price aren't surprised in the least when I let on that I'm leaving to test the waters of entrepreneurship. Plenty of portfolio managers have left to do their thing in the last two years, so I'm just part of an ongoing trend.

I tell the firm's muckety-mucks that I'm leaving after June 1983 and all the right words are uttered about how my service to the firm is appreciated and about how I'm grateful for the opportunity to have worked as a portfolio manager, which is true.

Even though we occasionally hear of spectacular ponzi schemes that defraud investors of millions and billions of dollars, the federal government has some incredibly stringent safeguards in place when it comes to preventing financial institutions from fleecing the public. In my view, one is the sheer volume of paperwork it takes to register a new money management company with the Securities and Exchange Commission (SEC).

During my final weeks with T. Rowe Price I basically have two jobs—the one that I perform for the firm during the day and the avalanche of SEC paperwork I tackle at night. Along with eight million forms, I have to fill out a narrative of my investment approach. Which is actually a useful exercise, because it causes me to think carefully and deeply about what my overriding philosophy will be.

Because I'm very valuation-conscious, I've come up with something that I call GARP, an acronym for *growth at a reasonable price*. That's as opposed to GAAP, which is *growth at any price*, or GASP, *growth at a silly price*.

To understand GARP, it's helpful to know that investment clients generally compare the performance of their portfolios to well-established financial benchmarks. Sometimes it's a broad market index such as the Standard & Poors 500, or it can be an index that's more representative of a manager's investment style.

Since Brown Capital Management will focus on growth-style investments, the performance index of choice will be one of the Russell series, which are pegged to a market capitalization assignment. For example, the Russell 1000 Growth Index is the benchmark of choice for a Large-Cap assignment.

For a Mid-Cap assignment, the Russell Mid-Cap Growth Index is used.

The foundation of Brown Capital Management's GARP investment style will be captured by three portfolio characteristic metrics. While each individual security may not adhere to all of these metrics, the group of holdings the portfolio is comprised of will.

When my team and I structure portfolios, we'll want to achieve the following, compared with the appropriate benchmark:

- Superior estimated long-term earnings growth
- Superior profitability, as measured by return on equity (ROE)
- A lower PEG ratio, which is a price/earnings (P/E) ratio based on the next 12 months' earnings to long-term estimated earnings growth

In a nutshell, GARP will be about paying less and getting more. It will also be about remaining faithful to the aforementioned portfolio characteristics, which should allow Brown Capital Management to outperform the relevant benchmark.

If the yardsticks I've laid out sound arcane or exotic, trust me, they're not. I'm using guidelines that are well-known to investment professionals—I'm just viewing them through a different prism than is customary.

Put in car enthusiast's terms, my firm's bread and butter will be stocks that sell at a Chevrolet Impala price point, but eventually perform with the robustness of a Ferrari Testarossa. Admittedly, companies with that kind of growth potential aren't lying under every rock. But they do exist, and my job will be to discover them with regularity and to line my clients' portfolios with them.

I have no doubt of my ability to do this, because I'm doing it day in and day out at T. Rowe Price.

Between my responsibilities at Price and the paperwork I owe the SEC, I've been getting about four hours of sleep daily as I wait for my time at Price to wind down. This isn't a complaint, because I'm so excited while tackling my Brown Capital Management duties after work that I have to make myself turn off the light in my study and go to bed.

Eventually my last day at work arrives and people are coming by my desk and shaking my hand and hugging me and wishing me well. And then I leave T. Rowe Price for a final time, feeling no sadness and no apprehension about the future, just a deep and abiding sense of satisfaction over what I've been able to accomplish for the firm and for myself. I can look back and say my tenure was an unqualified win/win for all involved.

Sadly, I'm T. Rowe Price's first African American professional to ascend to the level of portfolio manager, as well as the last.

After taking a weekend to relax and decompress somewhat, I segue into the next phase of my career, that of owning and growing Brown Capital Management. Building a financial management firm calls for tons of hard work, some luck, and an awful, awful lot of networking and prospecting for potential clients.

I'm going to address the networking and connecting part, but first I've got to get my office space in order. I pick out a nice office that has a spectacular view of a tranquil woodland setting in Baltimore County. It contains the bare essentials in terms of office equipment—a copy machine, a fax machine, and a business phone line. The commute is the best I've ever had, given that it's about 10 paces past my bedroom door, then about 20 more footsteps down the stairway of my home.

That's right, Brown Capital Management's very first office is in the study of my house. The nerve center of my fledgling financial empire makes me privy to the day-to-day interpersonal dynamics between my two teenage daughters and their mother, which can be a blessing or a curse depending on what family drama is playing out.

My new workplace is a few feet away from the kitchen, which I've sworn to steer clear of while working. The only heft I'm looking to generate, I remind myself, is in my billfold. So the refrigerator will remain off-limits . . . most of the time.

When most small businesses fail, one of the main reasons is a tendency to let expenses outstrip revenues early in the game. So I'm following a business plan that might be described as one of creeping incrementalism—a series of small forward steps that will be undertaken only when Brown Capital Management has the underlying financial resources to justify them.

Therefore, I don't have a fulltime attorney, or an accountant, on retainer yet. Nor do I even have stationery, although I plan to get some business cards and Brown Capital Management letterhead made soon.

Not having a high-rent office full of fancy furniture and equipment is the way to go—why bother when I don't have a single client yet?

Chapter 17

Everyone's Medical Nightmare

Today is Tuesday, July 5, 1983, the first day of business for Brown Capital Management, Inc.

The No. 1 song in the country is "Flashdance . . . What a Feeling" by Irene Cara, *Time* magazine has an "AIDS Hysteria" headline on its cover, and the Standard and Poor's 500 Index opened at 168.11 and closed at 168.64 on Friday, July 1, 1983, prior to the start of the long Fourth of July weekend.

It's a little bit before six o'clock, the sun isn't up, and I'm already in my study and at my desk, wearing a pair of casual slacks and a short-sleeve cotton shirt. I'm way too excited to still be lolling around in bed. What I'm feeling right now is probably akin to what eight-year-olds experience on Christmas Eve as they anxiously await the arrival of Old Saint Nick. I've been diligently, patiently training for this day for 15 years, beginning when I ditched my engineering career to get an MBA.

And I'm more than a little curious to see what the gods of high finance have in store for me and my venture.

As I putter about in my study, putting things in order, the rest of the Brown family begins trooping downstairs, beginning with Sylvia and followed by Tonya and Jennifer. Everyone sticks their head into my office and says good morning and wishes me well, a novel departure from the start of my workdays at T. Rowe Price.

After Sylvia feeds the kids breakfast and shuttles them off to their summer activities, I fully immerse myself in the routine of becoming a business mogul.

Before I left T. Rowe Price I mailed out hundreds of announcement cards to let business associates know that I was leaving to form Brown Capital Management. The mailing was a family affair, with everyone in Chez Brown stuffing announcements in cards and sticking stamps on them.

A few cards went to friends and acquaintances. But the lion's share went to trust and estate attorneys and CPAs that I've encountered over the course of a decade working at T. Rowe Price. The folks I've carefully targeted have clients that might be able to use my services.

So I pull out my Rolodex and start calling the individuals I've mailed cards to. Cold calling is way too hit or miss for me to be an effective use of my time, so I'm not going that route.

The target market I'm focusing on initially is wealthy individuals, small institutions, and small medical practices with retirement plans and pension plans that have a need to generate money. I've set my minimum investment amount at $100,000, which is a laughably low number in the financial management business.

But you make concessions like that when you're first starting out and desperately in need of clients.

The very first prospecting call I make as the owner of Brown Capital Management yields . . . nothing. Neither does the twentieth. Or the one hundred and twentieth. At least everyone that I've been getting in contact with remembers me, which isn't terribly difficult, given that I was the only African American at T. Rowe Price pursuing my line of work.

The bad news is, no one appears to be in the market for the financial services my new company is offering. That's okay. I hardly thought Day One would see me magically bring five new clients into the fold.

Basically, if I can secure my first client by the end of the week, I'll be overjoyed. In fact, if I can pull in *numero uno* by the end of my first month in business, I'll be grateful beyond measure.

So I'm far from discouraged or disappointed or frustrated to find that my solicitation efforts have garnered only rejection during my first day owning and running a financial management firm. I expected that and am more than willing to burn up my phone line for an entire year if that's what it takes to get my first client.

To break up the monotony of hearing "no" ad nauseam, I head into the kitchen and have lunch with Sylvia. She's back from dropping off our children and is making a conscious effort not to disturb me, even though she's curious how things are going. After a bite to eat, and a commiserative peck on the cheek from my wife, I leave the house and drive to my post office box, which isn't that far from my house.

The mail slot holds a single white business envelope that was originally mailed to Maryland Public Television, where "Wall $treet Week With Louis Rukeyser" is taped. The Maryland Public Television address has been blotted out with a fountain pen, and my post office box address has been jotted in. The letter appears to have originated in Washington, D.C., and was mailed by one Geraldine Whittington.

Clueless as to who that is, I shrug and take the letter back home to my study. When people go through the trouble of writing after having seen me on television, I feel the least I can do is dash off a paragraph or two to acknowledge their support.

So, I'll write Geraldine Whittington a short response and get back to getting in touch with prospects on my business line. I open Whittington's envelope and am relieved to pull out a letter with carefully executed cursive that's easy to read. Few things are worse than fighting your way through a letter with writing that looks like it was lifted from a doctor's prescription.

Whittington's letter starts out predictably—she's contacting me because she's watched me for a number of years on "Wall $treet Week With Louis Rukeyser." But in her second paragraph, the letter deviates in a most unexpected way: Whittington has come into a large sum of money from a medical malpractice settlement, and would like to know if I can recommend someone to manage her money?

Yes, yes, yes, I can definitely recommend someone!

Geraldine Whittington has conveniently left a contact telephone number in her letter, so I give her a ring. You can never be sure over the phone, but she sounds like an older woman who is well-educated, judging from her command of English. Miss Whittington seems genuinely startled that I've taken the trouble to call her and is thrilled to make my acquaintance, a development that never fails to amaze me, because I don't consider myself a celebrity.

"Miss Whittington, I'm pleased to meet you, too," I assure her. "Regarding your suggestion that I recommend someone to manage your money, well, I recommend myself! I've started a company called Brown Capital Management and this is my first day in business. Having you as a client would be a great way to start off as an independent money manager."

There's a brief moment of silence after I toss out my bold proposition. I can't vouch for what's happening on Miss Whittington's end of the line, but on my end I'm praying with every fiber of my being.

"I'm so happy to hear that you would be interested and available, because this is entirely new for me," she says finally. "I've never had this much money. Would you mind meeting with my attorney and my CPA, because they know a lot more about these matters than I do."

With those words, Brown Capital Management pulls in its first client, a wonderful woman who entrusts me with $200,000 of her money, because she senses that I'm trustworthy and dependable just from having watched me on television.

Turns out that Geraldine Whittington was President Lyndon Johnson's secretary. Her settlement stemmed from a surgical procedure that left her partially paralyzed on one side of her body.

On my first day as a money manager, I'm able to attract an account worth $200,000. Man, is life good or what?

"Sylvia! Sylvia!"

My spouse comes flying into my study and I sweep her off her feet before saying a word and give her a huge kiss.

"Number one is in the bag! I just got my first account, for $200,000! And the day's not even over yet. I should have started this firm a long time ago!"

Brown Capital Management gets its second client during my second week as a financial entrepreneur. You may recall that I made a decision not to go after any of T. Rowe Price's clients while I worked there?

I'm sure that being aboveboard with my former employers led to my second client, Jane Calhoun Bond, who had been a client of mine while I was with Price. She called my old employers asking how she could get in touch with me.

The folks at T. Rowe Price were kind enough to call my new business and relay Jane's contact information. You know darn well they wouldn't have been that accommodating if I had tried to take T. Rowe Price files or steal clients.

In fact, T. Rowe Price becomes a good referral source for me, because whenever they're contacted by someone who only wants to invest $100,000 or $200,000, they refer that person to me.

Jane Calhoun Bond opens an account for an amount substantially higher than the range I just mentioned, which gives me commitments well beyond $200,000 after just two weeks of operation. Interestingly, Jane and Miss Whittington both want to place their money under my management immediately, but I politely ask both to hold off for a brief period of time.

Once I get a proper office and at least one person to serve as a support staffer, I tell my new clients, then I'll put your money in a custodian account and get the ball rolling. Do I feel tempted to just snatch their money and fling it into a custodian account?

I'd be lying if I said no. But I'm determined to run my firm in a careful, fastidious way, and doing things correctly means not taking shortcuts.

Client No. 3 comes on board during my third week in business. He's Sylvia's brother, Charles Sparks Thurston, who's a dermatologist in San Antonio, Texas. Sparks, as Sylvia and I call him, has a small retirement plan worth $100,000 for his medical practice.

So now I'll have an amount under management that's in the high six figures as soon as I get my infrastructure properly set up.

At this point I need to tell you about a friend of Sylvia's, Ginny Tomlinson, who owns the Tomlinson Craft Collection fine crafts shop in Baltimore. This wise woman says she learned a valuable lesson not long after going into business—never judge people and their wealth based on appearance. Just assume that everyone who enters is capable of buying everything in the shop.

The parable of the fine crafts shop comes into play with Brown Capital Management's fourth client, who joined toward the latter part of August 1983.

He's the minister of my place of worship in Baltimore, Faith Presbyterian Church. I'd sent him an announcement card for my new firm, and he calls to congratulate me. My minister says he also wants to sit down in the next few days in order to discuss the services Brown Capital Management offers.

As he talks, I'm thinking: *I have a $100,000 minimum, and he probably wants to talk about $5,000!* I start to casually mention my minimum, but think about the fine crafts shop and hold my tongue.

When I eventually meet with my minister and his wife at their home, it turns out that the amount he has in his bank account, along with what the two of them own in jointly held securities, is well above my $100,000 minimum.

Bob lives very modestly, which made me erroneously assume that he's in the $5,000 investment range, when in reality he has a much, much higher amount to bring to Brown Capital Management. Lesson learned!

I haven't had a shingle out for two full months and it looks as though I'm going to have $1.7 million under management. Years down the road, that $1.7 million will fall well short of my subsequent $5 million investment minimum.

But a few weeks after starting my business, $1.7 million is manna from heaven, and I am incredibly grateful and humbled to have it. By the time August 27 rolls around, I have rented a small office in Baltimore and hired an administrative person.

In the midst of these developments, Sylvia performs a breast cancer self-exam after getting her annual checkup, and believes she's come across an abnormal lump. My spouse is trying to be calm and low-key about her discovery, but she's plainly terrified. Frankly, so am I.

Something is clenching and unclenching inside my abdomen as Sylvia talks about her disconcerting find. The last time I felt that horrible sensation was about 30 years ago, when a kind woman in South Carolina was giving my dying grandmother her last drink of water.

Sitting across the kitchen table from Sylvia, I take a breath and hold it for a millisecond before speaking. "It's probably nothing," I tell her in what I hope is a confident-sounding voice. "But you should let your doctor check it out."

"I already called him, Ed. I'm going on Friday."

That's three days from today. I spend the rest of the week praying and hardly thinking about Brown Capital Management at all. Unfortunately, what I'd desperately hoped would be nothing turns out to be a malignant tumor.

For once I am thankful that Tonya and Jennifer are heavily involved in extracurricular activities that keep them out of the house much of the weekend. We don't share Sylvia's devastating news with them initially, and arrange for friends who are parents to take over our chauffeur duties.

That enables Sylvia and I to spend most of Saturday and Sunday sobbing and holding each other, as we try to come to grips with a biopsy report that's everyone's medical nightmare.

Chapter 18

My Biggest
Business Mistake

Both of us are teary-eyed as Sylvia and I sit in her doctor's office, telling him we'd like to get a second opinion. Apparently he anticipated this request, because he's already arranged for a different physician, an oncologist, to examine Sylvia.

Unfortunately, the second doctor comes up with the same diagnosis. Namely, that my wife has breast cancer.

Naturally, the girls are stunned when they're told of this horrible turn of events. And while I put on a brave façade for them—and for Sylvia when I can manage—when I'm alone I just can't get the tears to stop. *How could this happen to my wife?*

To us?

When a cancer diagnosis is handed down to someone you love dearly, especially a spouse, it initially has an air of unreality about it. I guess that switching into quasi-denial mode is the brain's way of protecting itself. I find myself doing the denial dance for the better part of a week.

163

The other thing rattling through my brain is: *You've gone and leaped off a cliff and started your own business—can you still pull this off?* The doubt stems from the fact that I depend on Sylvia so much emotionally, and from the fact that she's also the number-one player in my support system.

But after spinning around and around in circles and experiencing major disorientation, I gradually begin to get a grip. We both do. There's nothing meek, retiring, or defeatist about my wife and I, and our natural inclination is to fight like hell against this cancer thing that's threatening our household.

Since I'm no longer an employee of T. Rowe Price, I have to make COBRA payments to extend my family's health care insurance. I take care of that, and then I get on the phone to one of Sylvia's brothers, Sparks, who was Brown Capital Management's third client.

Sparks is the oldest of the six Thurston siblings and he helps me wrap my brain around what might be the best medical course of action for his sister.

Sylvia opts for a mastectomy, and the surgeon who'll be performing the procedure explains to both of us how things will proceed. He also cautions us that we can expect a fairly lengthy recovery period, but adds that the odds of the cancer recurring are very small.

The operation goes without a hitch, and I'm pleased to note that my wife has been cancer-free in the intervening 28 years since her surgery.

What all this has taught me is that nothing is promised, so live every day to the fullest. One day you can be on top of the world, and the next you can find yourself knocked off your horse and wallowing in the dirt.

Those words are probably an abstraction for some people, mere ink printed on a page. Nothing makes you appreciate how precious life truly is until you're faced with a very real prospect of losing it.

      ★   ★   ★

When I was at T. Rowe Price, I would have run through a brick wall to be in a position to advance the fortunes of Brown Capital Management. But in light of the cancer scare my family has just weathered, it's taken me a number of weeks to recapture my energy and enthusiasm for entrepreneurship.

Rather than merely go through the motions following Sylvia's mastectomy, wasting my clients' time as well as mine, I put Brown Capital Management on temporary hiatus and focus on my most important priority at the moment—assisting my wife with her recovery.

Only after I'm certain that my wife is fully on the mend does my appetite for business gradually return. I'm surprised to learn this about myself. I'd always fancied myself a very compartmentalized person whose passions for family and business were spheres that functioned independently of one another.

Nothing could have been further from the truth. I'm pleased, and relieved, to discover that I'm a lot more compassionate and caring and empathetic than I thought.

Now it's time once again to see whether I can build a viable money management business.

I start going back to my base of operations, about 900 square feet of office space in downtown Baltimore, at 519 N. Charles Street, a four-story building I have an ownership stake in. Even though I didn't work any less diligently in my study than I do in my new office, my new digs do have a more business-like, professional feel.

Formerly occupied by an interior designer who's a friend, my office has a huge bay window with an impressive view of downtown and is also furnished and decorated in an upscale manner. Being downtown makes it possible for me to bring potential clients into my workspace, and easily meet business contacts for lunch downtown. Being downtown also makes it easy to travel to most of the business meetings I've been attending religiously.

My office is subdivided into two basic work areas, so basically one space is mine and the other is used by an account administrator I've hired, Millie Eckhardt, who used to work for T. Rowe Price. Millie does all the record keeping for clients and for Uncle Sam, and also handles all correspondence.

When I'm not out glad-handing and passing out business cards, I can usually be found at my desk, doing company research. I don't concentrate on mature companies such as Boeing and Coca-Cola and DuPont. They don't have the kind of growth potential I'm looking for, plus their stock is fairly expensive. There can't be growth at a reasonable price, the basic investment tenet Brown Capital Management was founded on.

I'm on the prowl for companies that will be future stock-market superstars, but for the time being are still somewhat early-stage, or are in the process of dramatically improving their management structure, or the products or services they offer to the public.

So I devote much of my day to poring over corporate earnings reports, SEC filings, and press clippings as I try to decipher whether the requisite ingredients are in place that will lead to sustained strong performance over a multi-year period.

I enjoy doing research, but my real passion is attracting new clients to Brown Capital Management, then putting together killer stock portfolios whose performance outstrips the market's. The other thing that floats my boat is artfully managing portfolios on a day-to-day basis. I don't want to manage people, per se, but when your name is on the front door, people management is unavoidable.

What's my hang-up with management? Simply put, I don't particularly care for confrontation, and will come to find that my biggest entrepreneurial shortcoming is a reluctance to hold employees to the same uncompromising standards I hold myself to. When I get around to lowering the boom, sometimes it's not in the timeliest possible manner.

However, that's not a problem now because the only employee I have is Millie Eckhardt. However, I could use someone who can serve as an analyst, and reach out to an old friend for help.

Bob Hall, who worked with me at T. Rowe Price, is starting to experience personality conflicts inside the firm he started with some other T. Rowe Price types. I've stayed in touch with Bob, and will be calling to see if he can recommend an analyst. At the end of the day, I would love to have Bob join my firm, after I have enough business to justify that move.

Speaking of T. Rowe Price, it's time for me to take the gloves off with them. I made a concerted effort not to leave with any of their clients. But now that I've been out for a few months, they're just another adversary in the financial-management jungle. One with a client I have my eyes on.

The account in question belongs to the Sisters of the Order of St. Benedict, a monastic community of Benedictine women founded in 1857 and located in St. Joseph, Minnesota. I had a very warm relationship with the group's treasurer, Sister Miriam, while I was with T. Rowe Price, so I call to see if she has any interest in transferring her multi-million dollar account to my firm.

"Ed, I would really like to work with you and with Brown Capital Management," Sister Miriam says, and she promises to run my proposal past her finance committee. When she gets back to me, it appears that reservations were voiced about the fact that I'm the only investment professional in my company.

However, I'm told that as soon as I hire another investment professional, the Sisters of the Order of St. Benedict are willing to consider switching from T. Rowe Price to Brown Capital Management.

Two seconds after my first investment professional comes onboard, you can bet I'll be on the phone to Sister Miriam, in St. Joseph, Minnesota.

When 1983 draws to a close I have $4.3 million under management. That number grows to $6.7 million by the last day of 1984 and $12.6 million by the end of 1985. In retrospect, I'm impressed with the progress Brown Capital Management made during those years. But when you're in the trenches battling on a daily basis, it's difficult to be detached or satisfied.

One thing that my efforts from 1983 through 1985 impressed upon me was that I would never reach my financial objectives by operating as a one-man band. It was time to take Brown Capital Management to the next level by hiring another investment professional. Hopefully during the first half of 1986.

That person turned out to be Roger Silver, who's balding and has prominent tufts of hair on both sides of his head. Soft-spoken and mild-mannered, Roger had done financial work with the state of Maryland pension fund before moving to a Baltimore investment firm as an equity manager.

Roger left the firm and opened an investment firm of his own in Baltimore. Unfortunately for Roger, he's been unable to pull a single client into his new investment firm, and has taken me out to lunch to pick my brain about ways to attract clients.

Roger invites me to lunch a second time and casually asks if I have any interest in taking on another investment manager at Brown Capital Management. Now Roger's mild demeanor and inability to generate business should set a sea of red flags fluttering. But in truth, he's caught me during a weak period, because I am more than a tad weary of running the entire show at my shop every day.

Plus I'd recently asked a T. Rowe Price portfolio manager if he had any interest in joining me, and he politely turned me down. Seemed the velvet handcuffs were a little too comfortable for him to seriously weigh rolling up his sleeves and helping to build an investment firm.

Naturally I perform my due diligence on Roger and hear positive things from everyone I ask about him. I even arrange for Roger to meet Sylvia and he passes her sniff test. So I bring Roger into the firm in May 1986.

Five minutes after he accepts my offer, I'm dialing the telephone number of the Sisters of the Order of St. Benedict, in St. Joseph, Minnesota. True to her word, Sister Miriam invites Roger and me to travel to St. Joseph to meet with her investment committee.

So we fly to Minnesota, make a presentation to the investment commitment and travel back to Baltimore. Literally the next day, the Sisters of the Order of St. Benedict hire Brown Capital Management to invest $5 million for them.

Roger hasn't been with me two weeks and already his presence has indirectly attracted $5 million to my company. Not bad. I view his hiring as an opportunity to add a seasoned investment professional at a very reasonable level of compensation.

Reasonable because I've made a deal with Roger to augment his salary with an equity stake in my company. The percentage he'll own will eventually balloon to 20 percent, because I'm not paying him a lot in cash. The idea is that if we're successful, Roger will do well. And he firmly believes that my reputation will allow us to boost Brown Capital Management into a position where shares of the company will be worth quite a bit.

This equity arrangement will turn out to be a massive miscalculation on my part. In fact, it's the biggest faux pas I've ever committed as a business owner.

However, in the short term, things are going pretty well. Not long after the Sisters of the Order of St. Benedict entrust me with $5 million, Coors and Monsanto each put about $5 million into my company. They contacted me as a result of searches they'd initiated, because a lot of companies are interested in having minority money managers invest segments of their capital. There aren't many black investment managers nationwide with my qualifications, so a fair number of those searches have ended up on my doorstep.

Unfortunately, that social experiment came to a screeching halt after Reagan took office, as if scads of minority money managers were going to be enriched as a result. But I was able to benefit before the brakes were applied.

As all this is taking place, I'm proud to note that I'm not giving short shrift to any of my responsibilities as a husband or father. I still go to church with my family every Sunday and have made every parent/teacher conference and PTA meeting for the girls. Plus, the four of us go on at least a couple of interesting vacations every year.

My love of real estate hasn't flagged one iota, either. Not only do I partly own the building that houses my office, but Sylvia and I are now the proud owners of a couple of apartment buildings and a carriage house in downtown Baltimore. Every one of our rental units is clean and in good repair—neither Sylvia or I have it in us to play slumlord.

Sylvia has been acting as the property manager for these holdings for several years, and has had her hands full dealing with maintenance issues, occupant complaints, and of course occasionally deadbeat tenants who produce some of the most heart-wrenching sob stories known to man.

I'm generally glad that neither Sylvia nor I are hard asses, but you can't have a good cop/good cop pairing when dealing with rental properties. Most tenants are dependable and mature, but the unreasonable ones are a chronic pain in the backside. There's no other way to put it.

The rental income these properties generate is welcome, but riding herd on them is starting to get very old for Sylvia. I think it's about time to put a professional property manager on the case.

Chapter 19

A Horror Movie
without Sound

Even though it's manmade, there are times when the stock market
can be every bit as unpredictable, intimidating, and unfathom-
able as forces of nature like hurricanes and volcanoes.

This morning is one of those times. Stock values that have been
painstakingly built over decades are going up in smoke in front of
my eyes, and for no apparent reason. I've seen bad markets before,
but nothing anywhere near as horrific as today's on Monday, October
19, 1987.

Stocks are imploding across the board, going to hell in a hand
basket and all the financial experts are ducking and scratching their
heads. I'm just as baffled and bewildered as anyone else, despite my
fancy Indiana University MBA and 17 years of experience in the
money management business.

What can I compare this to? Perhaps the best analogy is an
aviation accident—we're so used to seeing planes float safely across
the sky that if you ever saw a crash, the resulting flames, smoke, and
wreckage would have a surreal quality.

That's exactly how I feel in Brown Capital Management's little two-room office on Baltimore's Charles Street. My clients, my company, and even my own stock holdings are crashing and burning before my eyes and I'm in disbelief and powerless to do anything.

Well, that's not totally true—I could always join the mass panic and start dumping stocks left and right regardless of price, further fueling the freefall. But it doesn't make sense to me to sell into a market that's in the throes of such a ferocious downward spiral. No one has any inkling where bottom is for this stock-gobbling monster, which will come to be known as Black Monday.

Facing the options of doing nothing, or pulling my hair out and screaming and jettisoning every position I can get my hands on, I do nothing. I let this terrifying stock market anomaly run its course as I sit in the office with Roger and account administrator Donna Courtney, who will become Brown Capital Management's second-longest tenured employee after me.

On Black Monday, Donna, Roger, and I try to find words that adequately capture our incredulity as we numbly watch a gut-wrenching horror movie without sound.

Fortunately Roger is an unemotional sort, so he doesn't panic, either. I can't tell if he's silently, fervently praying for the madness to end and for stock prices to eventually return to normal, but I sure am!

God, please just grant me a soft landing. I knew there would be days like this, I just didn't think it would be this bad.

One of the oddest things about the stock meltdown is that the office phones are fairly quiet. By now Brown Capital Management has a fair number of institutional clients and wealthy individuals, and apparently all of them are too frightened and discombobulated to call.

Thank goodness for little miracles, because I'm not capable of explaining to them in a cogent, logical way what's happening. Nor do I have a single reassuring word that would be based on facts.

The only calls are from Wall Street brokerage firms, telling me what a bleak picture the market is painting, and how no one has a satisfactory explanation. Tell me something I don't already know.

Along with the fact that clients aren't calling, another saving grace is that I'm not fully able to keep track of the market and its various stocks. Nowadays I have scads of computers and online stuff and

Bloomberg machines and real-time stock news from markets around the world.

But on Black Monday, all I have is one hand-held device known as a Quotetrek. A little bigger than a calculator, it has a little stand and metal antennas that help it operate properly. I can only punch in one stock at a time and watch its price go down. Right now, I can't afford to buy or lease fancier equipment that can give me a more comprehensive sense of just how bad things are.

That's a good thing, because if I had the ability to sit here and watch an entire screen of my holdings nosediving in unison, I'd probably go nuts.

The torture of Black Monday finally comes to an end when the market finally shuts down at the end of an awful day where it plunges 22 percent. Not at all eager to stay late on this particular day, I lock up the offices of Brown Capital Management and drive home in an absolute daze.

Sylvia and I sit on the couch and watch as Black Monday dominates the TV news. My wife leans over and gently lays her head against my shoulder, the first good thing that's happened to all day.

"This is really awful, Eddie" she says in a consoling voice. "I'm so sorry you went through all that."

"Markets go up, markets go down," I tell Sylvia. "This one just went down more than anyone imagined. It's not the end of the world—life will go on."

That brave statement doesn't belie how incredibly nerve-wracking it is to think about what tomorrow may bring. Is this going to continue? And what in the world triggered all this craziness in the first place?

Hopeful that the following day doesn't morph into Black Tuesday, I'm at my desk by six, assessing the damage wrought by Black Monday. I start calling every one of my clients a few hours later, after checking to see how everyone's portfolio endured the previous day.

To my delight, Brown Capital Management portfolios went down significantly less than the market, including our pure equity accounts, which are comprised entirely of stocks. My calls to clients usually play out one of two ways, pointing up the different expectations investors bring to the table.

For institutional clients, relative performance rules the day. By that, I mean that institutional clients tend to measure investment performance relative to the market. If you can get their portfolios to outdo the market by 2 or 3 percentage points when the market is doing well, or when it's doing poorly, you've earned your money in their eyes.

This is because institutional clients are convinced that over the longer term, there will be a positive absolute return. They're also convinced that stocks will outperform bonds, and that bonds will outperform money market instruments.

Individual clients, on the other hand, tend to be relative during up markets—like institutional clients. But during down markets, individual clients tend to look at investing through an absolute prism. If the market drops 10 percent, and the portfolio they have with you only goes down 3 percent, individuals howl about the 3 percent they lost, while ignoring the additional 7 percentage point drop you shielded them from.

So that's how my phone calls are unfolding as I contact anxious and jittery clients in the wake of Black Monday. The institutional folks are praising me for not letting them feel the full brunt of the market's fury, while the individual clients are unhappy to have lost anything.

I believe in providing superior customer service, which is why I'm contacting each of my clients. But I have to draw the line at doing an excessive amount of hand-holding, because there are just too many demands on my time.

One individual investor that I call is a judge who has a balanced portfolio, meaning it's comprised of stocks and less volatile bonds. I'm actually kind of proud as I relate that his portfolio only went down 5 percentage points in the midst of an aberrational debacle that saw the market collapse 22 percentage points.

The judge is in no mood to hear about the 17 percentage points of additional pain he was spared—he lost $50,000 yesterday and was so upset last night that he sought refuge in his hot tub instead of going to bed.

I understand that when individual clients lose money, they're going to be upset. My own holdings got whacked on Black Monday!

But when the judge keeps going on and on and on, in an effort to make doggone sure that I feel his towering angst and anxiety, I politely excuse myself with a promise that I'll call back before day's end. I have other clients to reassure and can't devote a huge chunk of my morning to just one.

When I do get back to the judge, I strongly suggest that he sell all of his stocks after the market recovers, which I assure him it surely will in time. When he's fully recouped his loss from Black Monday, I advise the judge that it might be a good idea to create a low-risk portfolio comprised entirely of bonds. I also tell him that Brown Capital Management is not interested in managing pure fixed-income portfolios, and that he'll need to find someone to handle that for him.

You really do need to pick your clients carefully in this business. It's not that I don't feel for the judge and his position, because I do. But investors have to be big boys and girls and totally comprehend and appreciate the rewards and risks of investing. It's hardly as though I didn't lay out the full range of potential scenarios for the judge, as I do for all of my clients when they're first getting started.

Thankfully, Black Mondays don't roll around that often, but they can once every blue moon.

In light of my snap decision on Black Monday not to sell with the panicked herd, you may be wondering if that's my standard M.O. when a stock begins to dramatically falter. In a word, no.

When a stock goes down, its needs to go back up at a higher percentage than it went down just to get back even. That's why you really have to be careful about how much you allow a security to decline, because it becomes much more difficult to recoup that loss through an alternative investment.

For example, if a stock declines 10 percent, you have to be up 11 percent just to get back even. It's not additive, it's multiplicative. If you lose 20 percent, you have to be back up 25 percent. If you lose 30 percent, you have to be back up 43 percent. If you lose 50 percent, you have to be back up 100 percent.

At Brown Capital Management I have something called The Loss Curve that graphically demonstrates this principle. It's something that helps keep me mindful of the impact a declining stock can have on my clients, my company, and on me as an investor.

At the top of The Loss Curve it says, "Cut your losses before it's too late!" That's a reminder that my pain threshold is a 30 percent decline. That's the point at which I'll consider selling a security. That's not an absolute, but it will definitely be an option I'll be mulling at that point. Because, as I've already noted, the more you let a stock go down, the more difficult it becomes to recover.

The negative impact that The Loss Curve can wreak on my clients' portfolios and on my personal holdings is obvious. From a corporate standpoint, it's helpful to remember that my revenues are pegged to a percentage of the assets I have under management. If a particular security—or the entire market—takes a big tumble, that decline in assets represents an immediate decline in Brown Capital Management's revenues for the next quarterly billing cycle.

Keeping my hand away from the ejection seat handle and not haphazardly dumping stocks turned out to be the right thing to do on Black Monday. However, I also committed my biggest blunder as an equity manager that day.

The Friday prior to Black Monday, Brown Capital Management got a new institutional account that was funded entirely in cash. When the market crashed on Monday, I should have invested every cent into the market. Regardless of what happened next, I would have locked in a 22 percentage point advantage to the market, which is absolutely huge.

Instead I built the institution's portfolio the traditional way, by tiptoeing along and incrementally investing the institution's money over time. It was an opportunity lost, and definitely one of my dumbest investment mistakes. I could use the excuse of being shell shocked by the events of that day, except that's not an excuse.

Did I take any other lessons from Black Monday? Yes—that I never, ever want to experience anything remotely like it again.

Chapter 20

The Art and Science of Stock Picking

T here are nearly 14,000 publicly traded companies on the New York Stock Exchange and NASDAQ. How does Brown Capital Management winnow that down to only 40 to 65 individual securities that we choose to commit our clients' and investors' precious capital to?

Remember, our goal—and the expectation of our clients and investors—is two-fold over the long-term. The first objective is to produce an attractive positive absolute return consistent with their risk tolerance, while the second is to outperform the relevant performance benchmark.

As I walk you through the stock-picking process at Brown Capital Management, please refer to Figure 20.1, "Narrowing the Universe."

Let's start with how Brown Capital Management gets investment ideas. Fortunately, they come from a multitude of sources.

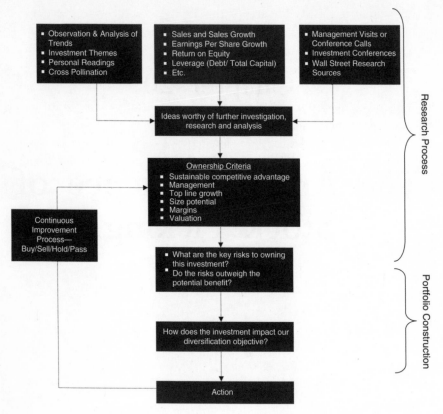

Figure 20.1 Narrowing the Universe from 14,000+ Companies to 40 to 65 Portfolio Holdings
SOURCE: Brown Capital Management

For one thing, we avidly read a number of publications, and some ideas spring to life as a result of the voluminous reading we do. Others stem from the fact that we're astute observers of broad trends in the economy and market segments, and also happen to be consumers ourselves who keep an attentive eye on what's transpiring in the marketplace.

We attend several investment conferences each year that enable us to meet the top managers of growth companies, which is always good for a potential investment gem or two. Lastly, Brown Capital

Management has at its finger tips the ability to screen large databases filling with selection criteria such as a minimum earnings growth, level of profitability, and so on.

Once we've amassed a few hundred potential stocks to invest in, then we delve into a segment of the selection process that's part art, part science. The six investment criteria noted in Figure 20.1 are used to evaluate each investment idea.

This is an art because unless you're actually privy to a company's inner workings, you can never be totally sure what takes place within its four walls, so solid intuitive and analytical skills are called for. It's part science, because we have a lot of concrete numbers—like those generated by income statements and balance sheets—to work with.

In the final analysis, successful investing calls for a combination of analytical skill, and good judgment. When the process plays out, the investment ideas left standing are the ones that Brown Capital Management invests in.

You will note that one of the hoops an investment idea has to jump through to become a Brown Capital Management pick is "attractive valuation." Our valuation methodology is a real differentiator for our firm, and contributes significantly to the performance numbers we've managed to generate.

Consistent with our growth at a reasonable price (GARP) investment approach, it is critical to determine how much to pay for growth. Our proprietary "Valuation Methodology," which can be found in Figure 20.2, provides guidance in that regard.

Estimated five-year earnings-per-share growth rate is along the horizontal axis, and price/earnings (P/E) ratio based on the next 12 months' estimated earnings is along the vertical axis. Many growth managers operate in a linear manner, that is, along the upward sloping straight line in the graph.

By contrast, how much we are willing to pay for growth in terms of P/E is dependent on the interest rate environment. Our valuation methodology establishes a required rate of return for each security based on the riskiness of the investment and the level of interest rates, utilizing the five-year U.S. Treasury bond rate as

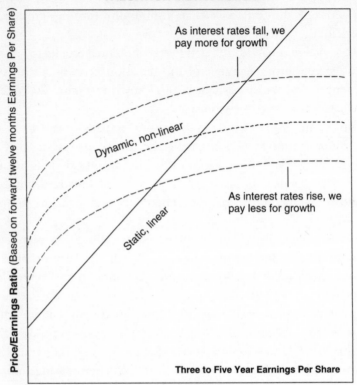

Figure 20.2   Valuation Methodology
SOURCE: Brown Capital Management

the "riskless asset," and company specific risk premiums for each security.

The bottom line, as is evident from the exhibit, is that we operate more in a curvilinear manner. We are willing to pay a much higher P/E for a given growth rate in a low interest rate environment, and a much lower P/E for that same growth rate in a higher interest rate environment.

Chapter 21

"God, I Owe You One!"

I swear to you that I'm not a thrill seeker.

I just happened to have gravitated to a business that can be volatile every now and then. And I like flying planes strictly because of the intellectual challenge involved, and because flying is a time-saver. I *love* fast cars, too.

But I'm not a thrill seeker . . . or at least I don't think I am. Sylvia, on the other hand, might disagree vehemently. Never ask my wife if she's ever been at death's doorstep, because she'll gleefully point to two occasions: A rollercoaster ride during her youth and a plane ride with her adventurous husband.

The latter incident involved a trip from Baltimore to Allentown, Pennsylvania, to see my mother. Let me preface this story by telling you that when the FAA certifies pilots to fly airplanes, there's a licensing classification that says you can fly only if you can see where you're going, and there's a more advanced certification that enables you to navigate in bad weather and in clouds by using your instruments.

I'm certified to fly VFR, which stands for visual flight rules. Flying VFR at night is not a problem, as long as it's a clear night without a lot of clouds or fog, and as long as a flight instructor has cleared you to fly at night. I've started working on my instrument rating, but haven't quite finished it yet.

The aircraft my wife and I are to fly to Allentown is a single-engine, four-seat Cessna 172 that I've rented from a local flying club. It has a four-cylinder gasoline powerplant, will do about 140 mph, and can't fly any higher than 13,500 feet. A teeny, very forgiving aircraft that lets every little gust of wind blow you around, the Cessna 172 is perfect for a fairly inexperienced pilot who has a little over 100 hours of flight time. Like me.

I am darned proud as I pull back on the control yoke and the Cessna lifts into the sky. I steal a glance at my wife and can see she's enthralled to be looking at Baltimore-area landmarks from a whole new vantage point.

Wearing a light green headset with a microphone and stylish aviator dark shades—what pilot would be caught dead without them?—I don't have the luxury of sightseeing as I talk to air traffic control, scan the sky for other aircraft and simultaneously keep an eye on my instruments.

I'm cleared to ascend to an altitude of 6,500 feet, and that's where Sylvia and I putter along for a little over an hour, Allentown only 150 miles from Baltimore. I fly my final approach into Allentown's airport and I land the Cessna 172 with a smoothness, and precision, that I'll hold up to any Boeing 747 captain.

"That was fun, Eddie," Sylvia tells me as we slowly turn off the runway and onto a taxiway. My wife thinks I didn't see that little admiring look she shot me, but I did. It was worth the price of renting the Cessna 172, as well as the price of the aviation gas needed for this trip.

From Allentown's airport the two of us catch a cab to my mother's and the three of us have a tremendous time sitting around talking and laughing and catching up. We're having so much fun, in fact, that I've stayed an hour and a half longer than I intended. Meaning that as we're flying back to Baltimore, nightfall will catch us before we land.

That's a bit of a problem, because I've never landed a plane at night before. *How in the world could I put myself AND my wife in this kind of predicament?*

What had been a leisurely, carefree little jaunt has turned into a pressure-filled situation that will severely test my limited experience as an aviator. Irritated as hell with myself, I keep remembering a placard I'd seen in an aviation unit during my Army days: "Superior pilots use their superior judgment to stay out of situations that call for their superior skill."

As the little Cessna drones along in the steadily darkening sky, Sylvia has an aviation map spread in her lap that I'm trying desperately to read. Because I'm only VFR-certified, I need to use the map in conjunction with ground landmarks, an increasingly difficult task in the fading light.

I can feel little tinges of panic tightening my neck and shoulder muscles, because I'm not exactly sure I can navigate my way to Baltimore Washington Airport tonight, much less the runway I'm supposed to land on.

Air traffic controllers at major airports can be snappish with pilots who sound indecisive or unclear about what it is they're trying to do, because that controller is juggling scores of aircraft at any given time.

Being an engineer, I know how fast I'm flying and I know my heading is correct, so I'm guessing that I should be about 25 miles from the BWI's control tower. The controller has me change my altitude and heading slightly, so I'll be properly aligned for my final approach.

After about a minute or so, he comes back on the radio.

"Cessna two-niner bravo, tango, do you see the runway."

"Negative."

So he has me climb to another altitude and heading to get me out of the way of other incoming traffic. After three more attempts to land, including one where a commercial jet is on my tail, I hear a very stern, no-nonsense voice in my headphones.

"Look straight ahead. You'll see some green landing lights. That's the center of the runway. Do you copy?"

Because I've never landed at night, it's pretty difficult to judge my distance from the ground as I descend. Consequently, the Cessna

172 comes down with a jolt that sends it bouncing roughly down the runway before I'm finally safely on the ground. Without having to look, I know doggone well there's no admiring expression following that ugly landing.

I manage to stay pretty cool throughout, but during the ride home the full impact of what could have happened to Sylvia and I hits me. *God, I owe you one after tonight.*

"I was okay in the plane but now that it's after the fact, I'm nervous as heck," I tell Sylvia, who's already pledged to never accompany me on another flight. "I don't understand that."

"You should understand it," my wife shoots back. "You have no business being up there!"

Can't argue with that one.

I fly a handful of times after that, just to prove something to myself, but within a few months I hang up my headphones and leave my flying to professionals who do it day in and day out.

Flying is one of those things you have to do regularly to remain proficient and safe. But when you fly for a few hours at a time every few months, like I do, you're basically tempting fate.

If there's a silver lining, along with the fact that I've escaped with my hide intact, it's that whenever I compile a bucket list, I won't need to jot down "earn pilot's license."

Chapter 22

Impressive Progress, Baffling Lethargy

I get my first major pension fund, which brings $20 million from the Dow Chemical Company, in 1990. The funny thing is, I nearly have to be hogtied and dragged to the meeting that eventually leads to this wonderful windfall.

Jack Wentworth, the dean of the business school at Indiana University—my alma mater—has asked me repeatedly if I would serve on a dean's advisory board he's put together for the business school. I keep begging off with the excuse that I'm trying to build and sustain Brown Capital Management. Well, actually, that's not an excuse—it's the truth.

Fortunately for me, he's insistent and calls back to read a partial list of the heavy hitters on the advisory panel, people like the chairmen of Ford Motor Company and Dow Chemical. Didn't take me long to change my tune about sitting in such august company. Corporate bigwigs like those are exactly who I need to be hobnobbing with to get business.

When the meeting gets underway, I find myself seated beside Frank Popoff, Dow's chairman, as well as the chair of the advisory board. Frank gives me the name of the person managing Dow's pension fund and tells me to call.

When I do, I get a song and dance about how the pension fund employs an incredibly rigorous process to select its investment managers, and how Dow has been working with one manager for more than 40 years and hasn't hired a new one in at least a decade.

But it's amazing how dramatically things can change when you know the right people. During the next advisory board meeting for Indiana University's business school, Frank Popoff asks me how my meeting with Dow went. When I tell him, Frank promises to look into the situation after he gets back to Dow.

Lo and behold, within a month's time I have $20 million from Dow's pension fund. And that definitely would not have come to pass without my Indiana University connection.

There's absolutely, positively, unequivocally no question that in the investment field, success is twinned to what you know, as well as who you know.

By the way, that $20 million represents Brown Capital Management's largest account to date. And this probably goes without saying, but now when I'm asked to sit on a board, instead of automatically saying "no" I first do a little investigating to see who's on the board.

The same year that I get the Dow account, 1990, I nail down $40 million from the California Public Employees Retirement System (CalPERS). After traveling to Sacramento, I only have 10 minutes to persuade CalPERS's investment committee why they should fund Brown Capital Management, a nerve-wracking experience detailed earlier in this book.

There's no question that 1990 is a watershed year for my company. To my way of thinking, it's the year that Brown Capital becomes a bona fide financial firm that's a permanent part of the investment industry's landscape. We're the real deal now!

Assets under management double from roughly $60 million to $120 million. We also have the largest public pension fund in the United States, in terms of assets. If anyone had predicted that accomplishment seven years ago when I started my company, I would have laughed in their face.

Getting a brand new investment firm to a point where it's operating at a high level is kind of a chicken-and-egg kind of proposition—people are reluctant to hire you unless you can demonstrate you have a fair number of clients.

So through most of 1990 I've been on a continual quest to attract clients and have been prospecting nonstop. But now, potential clients are starting to seek me out. When you pass the $100-million mark in assets under management, people tend to look at you differently.

And when you've gotten your clients a 14.72 percent rate of return for 1989, or can show a 11.01 percent annualized rate of return for your first five years in operation, that gets folks' attention, too.

For about a year now, we've been in a larger suite of downtown Baltimore offices, located at 809 Cathedral Street. I'm thinking seriously about expanding my staff, which is kind of a double-edged sword. On the one hand, when you start hiring folks, you obviously have a thriving concern.

But on the other hand, I started Brown Capital Management to manage investments, not people. That's why the thought of guiding a huge financial juggernaut with thousands of employees has never enthralled me. However, I'm definitely aiming to have billions of dollars under management.

With Brown Capital Management having turned the corner, so to speak, I continue to work my tail off to propel it to even greater plateaus. Unfortunately, that's not an ambition embraced by the firm's other investment professional, Roger Silver.

Now that Dow and CalPERS are onboard, Roger apparently is under the impression that we're on easy street.

He's earning a substantial amount of money now, I guess more than he ever dreamed of making, and that seems to have extinguished every bit of his fire and drive. It's crystal clear to me that Roger has zero desire to move beyond status quo.

It's also clear that his cruise-control approach is going to be a major problem for me moving forward. I'm doing most of the work now and he's sort of laying back, enjoying the fruits of what's already been accomplished. That's not acceptable.

In 1991 I start a new a new investment service focusing on small emerging growth companies, and Roger is not at all encouraging about the prospect of that succeeding. I don't think his reluctance is the result of rigorous analysis on his part—I simply think he's not interested in rolling up his sleeves and doing the heavy lifting necessary to get the new investment service established.

So for a second time I reach out to Bob Hall, who was my colleague at T. Rowe Price. I have two goals in mind. The first is to see if Bob will help me identify someone who can handle my proposed investment service. The second is to eventually lure Bob into my shop on a fulltime basis.

Bob agrees to come in as a three-day-a-week consultant, and with his help I hire Keith Lee to oversee the small company effort. This will turn out to be a truly pivotal hiring.

The second part of the equation falls into place when Bob agrees to join my firm. Seven years older than I am, Bob was also an engineer—mechanical—before coming into the investment business. Thanks to our very similar backgrounds and personalities, I not only consider him one of my most trusted colleagues, but also one of my dearest friends.

Like Keith, Bob is still with Brown Capital Management.

I still need to solve my dilemma with Roger, though. One day an account administrator comes scrambling out of Roger's office white as a sheet, reporting that she entered Roger's office to find him stretched out on the floor, apparently deceased or unconscious. After the startled young woman screamed, Roger arose from his slumber, causing her to bolt out of his office and into mine. It's time to confront this situation with Roger once and for all.

The solution turns out to be a win/win for everyone. Having foolishly put myself into a situation where Roger owns 20 percent of Brown Capital Management, I basically buy back his shares at a nominal price that's infinitely cheaper than the tens of millions of dollars it would have cost if I had waited years later.

Roger's happy to get the money and I'm ecstatic to once again be a sole owner. As part of the buy-back arrangement, I also get Roger to sign a sunset clause that makes his continued employment subject to my review at the end of each calendar year.

That lights a bit of a fire under Roger, who continues to work at Brown Capital until 1995.

About 10 years later, I learn from Roger's wife that he's passed away following a lengthy battle with cancer. She tells me that he was diagnosed with the disease right around the same time he became so bafflingly lackadaisical and lethargic at Brown Capital Management.

However, Roger Silver chose to keep his health crisis a private matter. Proving once again that there are times when appearances can be quite deceiving.

Chapter 23

To Heir Is Human

Any successful entrepreneur with intelligent, capable, responsible offspring has at one point or another contemplated passing the business along to their progeny.

Either Tonya or Jennifer have the ability to keep Brown Capital Management a viable, thriving enterprise if they focus their considerable talents and intellects on that objective.

However, Tonya is who I want to take over in the event that I retire, become incapacitated, or pass away.

Jennifer, a fireball whose personality is reminiscent of Sylvia's, has a bachelor's degree in economics and women's studies from Lehigh University, a master's in social work from Florida International University, and a doctorate in psychology from the University of Miami. Jennifer made it clear early on that she had no desire to become a businesswoman or to work with Brown Capital Management.

I respect that stance and have no qualms with it.

Tonya, who's three years older than Jennifer, has a personality more like mine in that she's somewhat reserved and is a very methodical planner. After getting a bachelor of science in math from Oberlin College and a bachelor of arts in music composition from the Oberlin Conservatory of Music, Tonya got an MBA from Harvard. She also got something of a personality overhaul at Harvard Business School, and transitioned from being somewhat shy and acquiescing to forceful and assertive.

Both Sylvia and I were very surprised, and pleased, by this transformation.

Prior to Harvard, Tonya did something that made me regard her not only as a beloved daughter, but also as a potential heir apparent to Brown Capital Management—she entered the investment business without any prodding from me!

Well, to be totally accurate I did play an indirect role in that decision. Because back when Tonya was a junior in high school, she and her classmates have to spend two weeks working in an area where they think they may want to pursue a career.

She asks if she can do her two weeks at Brown Capital.

"Absolutely not!" I tell her. "You have to do this on your own, not under my wing!" I only want Tonya at Brown Capital if she's seriously focused on joining the business, not just to satisfy some class assignment.

So I call a friend at Alex Brown & Sons named Al Berkley who's able to get Tonya exposed to all facets of the investment business. Al's so impressed with Tonya's knowledge of computers and spreadsheets that he hires her for the summer and pays her out of his own pocket!

Tonya also works at Alex Brown & Sons during her summer breaks while doing her undergraduate work at Oberlin.

At this point, a former colleague of mine from my days at T. Rowe Price, investment executive Tom Barry, enters the picture. Tom, who is a family friend, has been in Manhattan for several years as president of Rockefeller Company, which manages the Rockefeller family's wealth.

Tom also sits on Alex Brown's board and during one of his trips to Baltimore for a board meeting he runs into Tonya. After getting caught up, he asks what Tonya plans to do after graduating from Oberlin, and mentions that she may want to consider coming to Manhattan and working for him.

After Tonya graduates, Tom hires her and strongly suggests that it may be a good idea for her to consider getting a Harvard MBA.

You can't believe how happy these developments make me, because I've never actively tried to steer either of my children toward business, or toward the investment world. Okay, maybe there was a little telekinesis involved, but I swear I never bent Tonya's ear along the lines of, "I'd love to see you do this!"

She just seems to be following in my footsteps of her own accord! And if I had scripted the best possible path to prepare her to take over the business, I couldn't have done a better job. Math degree, investment training, Harvard MBA—Wow! I must be living right.

I rest easy at night knowing that one day Tonya will be running the show. In fact, on more than one occasion during private moments with Sylvia, I've turned to her and said: "This is what I have prayed for—it appears that I might have a successor!"

Oddly, I feel a slight twinge of envy when Tonya walks across the commencement stage at Harvard to accept her MBA. Not only do I find Ivy League schools fascinating, as I've already stated, but I wish I had graduated from one.

Not because I think I would have been one iota more successful, but because when you drop the Harvard, Yale, or Princeton name on someone, there's an automatic assumption that you've interacted with the best professors, curriculum, and students in the country. It's presumed that you can hit the ground running in highly competitive environments.

At least now I can be an Ivy Leaguer vicariously through my daughter, the future president and CEO of Brown Capital.

After Harvard, Tonya goes back to work for Tom Barry for about a year and a half, before he forms an investment company called Zephyr Management.

When Tonya and my future son-in-law, Kempton Ingersol, move to Dallas, Tom sublets office space in Dallas for Tonya, allowing her to help Zephyr Management make inroads into the Latin American market, beginning with Mexico.

Kempton—who today works for Brown Capital Management—finds work with a Dallas investment firm. Giving me a daughter who's my heir and a potential son-in-law who's also in the same business.

To make a long story short, I'm eventually able to have Tonya do some marketing work for Brown Capital on a consulting basis. In 1996, during a meeting with members of Brown Capital Management's brain trust that takes place in Palm Beach, Florida, Tonya stuns me by announcing that she's going back to school to get a master's degree in fine art.

For a couple of seconds I sit dumbfounded in the Palm Beach conference room where everyone is assembled, before finally managing to croak—"Wait a minute! What does that have to do with investments?"

And my beautiful firstborn sits there and stares back at me calm as can be and says, "Nothing. I'm going to become an artist. A painter."

I keep waiting for peals of laughter, followed by April Fool! even though it's the middle of summer. But none of that ever comes. After about a minute or so, it begins to dawn on me that Tonya is *actually serious about this!!!!*

And is never going to work shoulder-to-shoulder with me at Brown Capital, much less eventually run it.

After six years of preparing herself by working in the investment field, and taking two years to earn a Harvard MBA, my daughter is turning her back on my company to become an artist. What can you do when a child springs a devastating surprise like that on you?

What I do is spend the following two weeks in glum denial. Tonya's bombshell has badly upset the natural order of things in my neat little universe. I know you're supposed to let your children make their own decisions and not force your preferences on them . . . but my daughter's succession had been almost preordained, to my way of thinking.

Not only am I baffled by her rejection—and I know of no other way to term it immediately after her decision—but I'm deeply hurt by it.

Sylvia says that mine and Tonya's personalities are so much alike that we would have wound up butting heads anyway, and would have constantly placed Sylvia in the awkward position of playing peace-keeper/referee.

As the pain subsides with the passage of time, I have to grudgingly admit there's probably more than a kernel of truth to Sylvia's assessment.

To this day Tonya and I have never sat down and had a heart-to-heart about her decision, which in retrospect I've come to admire greatly. She knew I would be wounded, but also knew that she had to be true to herself, not her father's dream of how the world should be. Looking back, I can appreciate how incredibly difficult things must have been for Tonya, as well as how much courage it took to do what she did and how she must have agonized over things.

And I sincerely hope that the six years she spent in the investment business, and her efforts to earn an MBA, were because that's what she genuinely wanted to do, not because she was trying to please Dad.

As for the succession issue, when the time is right the leadership baton at Brown Capital Management will be handed to Keith Lee, who's currently managing director/senior portfolio manager. Keith is like a son to me, so in a manner of speaking I still get to pass the company along to one of my kids.

When Tonya decided to follow her artistic muse, she spoke to Keith confidentially about the reasons underlying her decision, with the proviso that he not share details with me. It says a lot about Keith and his character that he's never uttered a single word about that conversation . . . but any time you're ready to give up the skinny, Keith, I'm all ears.

Chapter 24

Anyone Care for a Can of New Coke?

Sometimes, being wildly successful in business can be extremely dangerous, even deadly.

That's because there can be a temptation to say, "Wow, look at how great we are. We must be doing something right!" Leading to complacency and a lack of innovation that can hamstring, or kill, a company.

So Brown Capital Management's prosperity in the late 1990s and beyond tests my leadership skills in unexpected ways. The electric do-or-die urgency that permeated the firm as a start-up is long gone. In its place is an undercurrent of pride, and even cockiness, stemming from Brown Capital's sustained ability to outperform the market.

Cockiness and confidence are fine with me as long as they don't morph into hubris, and an attendant sense that our continued success is pretty much preordained.

I guard against this in part by working just as hard, and as late, in 1999 as I did in 1983, and making doggone sure that my investment professionals and support staff notice. Plus I hire highly motivated, smart people and I ensure that they enjoy benefits and revenue-sharing plans that are equal to, if not better than, those found at larger investment houses.

A perk I've allowed myself is signing a contract in 1995 with NetJets, a fractional jet ownership company owned by Berkshire Hathaway. I dress simply, don't drive extravagant cars, and live in the same modest Baltimore County house Sylvia and I built in 1977. Private jet travel is my one indulgence, and I take advantage of it for business as well as trips with my family to residences we have in Florida and in Maine.

But success hasn't gone to my head. I think most of my close friends would tell you that the same Eddie Brown they knew in college or the Army is the same guy who owns an investment firm managing billions of dollars.

One area where I'm particularly proud of my leadership at Brown Capital Management is in the area of technology. As the firm has gotten more prosperous, I've made it a point to always stay ahead of the curve when it comes to technologic infrastructure. People couldn't believe the accounting and computer systems and databases and software we've had over the years.

Part of this is because I'm definitely a gadget person. But it's mainly because information is power in the investment business, and I want to ensure that we have plenty of power to go around inside Brown Capital Management.

★   ★   ★

Reacting to sales inroads from archrival Pepsi-Cola, in 1985 the Coca-Cola Company decided to mess with the soft drink that made it a prosperous brand that's recognized and coveted around the globe.

The iconic taste of Coca-Cola was reformulated into a sweeter concoction that was touted as "New Coke." I'm sure innumerable business school case studies have been written about Coke's bold move, which turned out to be one of the more spectacular marketing disasters in the annals of capitalism.

I bring up New Coke to highlight the fact that sometimes successful companies lose sight of the principles and products that made them thriving, viable concerns in the first place. That's precisely what happened to Brown Capital Management from 2004 to 2007. The poor relative investment performance experienced during this time frame can't be blamed on external factors such as the dot-com bust or 9/11.

The simple, unassailable fact is that, for four long years, we were simply our own worst enemy as we groped about blindly in the wilderness. Brown Capital Management lost sight of the strengths that had allowed us to accrue billions of dollars under management, and we paid dearly for it.

And as founder, president, and CEO, I take sole responsibility for the firm's painful New Coke era. I should have yanked down the curtain and I failed to. It goes without saying that I sincerely believed that what took place inside Brown Capital Management from 2004 through 2007 was in the best interest of our clients. It wasn't.

The root of the problem goes back to a trend that rippled through, and fundamentally reshaped, the investment business around the time of the dot-com bust. Questionable business practices began to become commonplace occurrences back then, such as Internet companies that were getting billion-dollar capitalizations, yet had no—or very small—revenues!

The new master in the investment business came to be short-term performance, and the new religion was a slavish devotion to stock market benchmarks and the computer programs that tabulate them. The other major development to come out of this time frame was an increased tendency among institutional investors to choose investment firms based on the recommendations of consultants, instead of on research performed independently by the institutions.

Brown Capital Management got caught up in this investment industry new think, instead of harkening back to the things we'd learned in business school and over nearly two decades of generating excellent returns for our clients.

My thinking as I went along with the new way of doing things was: *See, we're not hidebound—we're versatile and flexible enough to adapt to a rapidly changing landscape.* I wonder if lemmings think those same thoughts right up to the moment of impact?

Instead of clinging to our long-term focus when we're analyzing companies where we may want to allocate our clients' precious capital, a performance mantra that emphasizes a stock's performance over a five-year period, Brown Capital began focusing on performance results over three years, and in some cases as ridiculously short as 12 months.

That threw us off our game in terms of how we traditionally evaluate companies, and as a result we made some poor stock selections. That led to modest portfolio underperformance in 2004 and 2005, and significant underperformance in 2006 and 2007.

Having stocks remain in portfolios for shorter periods of time led to much higher portfolio turnover, which caused Brown Capital Management to lose some clients who were rightfully agitated by the performance numbers they were seeing.

After four years of serving my own brand of New Coke and hoping it will eventually become an acquired taste for my investors and for my firm, I've finally had enough and take it off the menu.

I order Brown Capital Management to return to the basics that made us great investors in the past, before we allowed pressure from consultants, clients, and Wall Street to ruin our formula.

We go back to good fundamental analysis and research, and return to focusing on companies that will yield impressive portfolio performance over the long term. I also tell my staff that we will stop putting too much stock in various market benchmarks—we're going to return to being agnostics, as had been the case in the past.

You've probably already surmised the moral to this whole episode, but I'm going to articulate it anyway—if it ain't broke, don't fix it. Also, go with your gut and stick with the stuff that made you successful in the first place.

I should point out that the aforementioned developments apply specifically and uniformly to our Large Cap investment service.

Before we look at how Brown Capital Management has done subsequent to 2007, it's helpful to understand that the firm has three broad categories of services: Domestic, which is comprised of companies domiciled inside the United States; International, which covers companies outside the United States; and Global, which is a mix of Domestic and International.

Within our Domestic category, there are four distinct investment services. The headings for three of them are: Small Company, Mid Cap, and Large Cap. A fourth, the All Cap Concentrated service, is concentrated in the sense that we will own no more than 20 to 25 security holdings, regardless of market cap.

What's our performance been like since that painful 2004 to 2007 period, when Brown Capital Management veered off the road, so to speak?

Given that the post-2007 world takes in the worst market decline since the Great Depression, the answer to that question is best judged by relative, rather than absolute, performance.

Brown Capital Management has slightly outperformed the relevant performance benchmark for our Large Cap International investment services, and has substantially outperformed the benchmarks for our Mid Cap, Small Company, and Concentrated All Cap Domestic investment services.

We learned from our mistakes, took the appropriate corrective action, are delighted by our performance turnaround, and are convinced we are back on the right track.

More importantly, our clients are pleased.

At the same time, Brown Capital Management has also seen more interest in our investment services from prospective clients and investors, which has resulted in significant new business and assets under management growth.

Epilogue

I'm sometimes asked why I continue to actively lead Brown Capital Management after having celebrated my seventieth birthday in November 2010. The reason is simple—because I find it immensely enjoyable, and always have.

There's no reason to give up something I find pleasurable, stimulating, and gratifying simply because of some arbitrary chronological milestone. As for retirement, I'll take my cue from Brown Capital Management colleague Bob Hall—who turns 78 in 2011.

In all seriousness, I've got 41 years of investment experience to draw from, I work in one of the most fascinating fields known to man, and I have the energy of a man in his fifties.

Plus, the thrill of showing up every morning at a thriving business concern that my vision, hard work, technical expertise, people skills, and hard-headedness made possible is indescribable.

Anyway, I seriously doubt Sylvia's ready for me to be puttering around our house on a daily basis.

The other thing that I'll be doing for the foreseeable future, in conjunction with Sylvia and our daughters, Tonya and Jennifer, is continuing to pursue philanthropic projects that pique our interest.

When sizing up the life and career I've been fortunate enough to enjoy, I often think back to Louis Rukeyser's observations when I was inducted into the "Wall $treet Week With Louis Rukeyser Hall of Fame" in 1996:

"This is truly a story in the most heart-warming tradition of the American Dream. Born in rural Florida to a dirt-poor 13-year-old mother, he has become one of the most eminent and trusted leaders in the world of investing . . .

His achievements would be memorable even if his story were not so inspiring. With brilliance and character, he has demonstrated to anyone who did not realize it long ago that the only race that matters in the quest for financial security is the race for sound advice.

And that the contestants in that race are properly judged not in black and white, but only in green and silver. He is a great American investor and it is a pleasure to welcome to our Hall of Fame, Eddie C. Brown. . . ."

Index